The Safe Haven

Scriptural Reflections for the Heart and Home

The Liturgical Season of Lent

M.C. Holbrook

ISBN: 9798863417288

DEDICATION

To Jesus, who transformed my trials into teachers and my home into a safe haven; to my husband Craig, who has been unwavering and steadfast in his call to guard our home; to the parents who have gone before us, passing onto us the secret treasures of our Catholic faith, and to the ones still here to support us; to each of my ten children: Jimmy, Krissy, Andrew, Eric, Katie, Grace, Michael, Isabella, Jack and Patrick, you are each the apple of my eye … and finally, to my "Casserole" prayer group: Christie, Gina, Kate and Suellen, without whom I would not have had eyes to see.

I love you all.

CONTENTS

FOREWORD

In January of 2020, I and two other women at my church were asked to give a talk to parents of children enrolled in the Religious Education program at our parish. The subject was prayer. I don't remember all the details of what we touched on, but there's one thing that stands out in my memory very clearly. I remember telling the audience that I did not have the gift of understanding Scripture. Oh, I believed with my whole heart that such a gift existed. And I faithfully practiced reviewing the daily liturgical readings each morning, at the predawn hours of the day. It's just that without my companion books to draw out the richer meaning of the text … I was a little lost. Or perhaps bored. I never understood how St. Therese of Lisieux could say that the only spiritual reading she ever needed was the Bible.

Now I do.

Shortly after my talk at the parish, the pandemic hit, and my routine of daily Mass came to an abrupt halt. It had been my lifeline for 20 years … How would I do life without it now? But Jesus gave me a grace I would never have discovered if it had not been for the isolation that came with COVID-19. He gave me the gift of his W ord which "in the beginning was with God, and … *was* God" (John 1:1). I *was* indeed receiving Jesus each day, chewing on him, becoming a part of his heart as he became a part of mine. Without that time of isolation, I would never have known and loved Jesus the way I do now. So thank you, Jesus, for turning my trials into teachers and my confinement into a cloister. Knowing what I know now, I would not change anything, even if I could. This is the miracle of *sub specie aeternitatis*: the perspective that views all things in the context of eternity.

> *Have no anxiety at all, but in everything, by prayer and petition, with thanksgiving, make your requests known to God. Then the peace of God that surpasses all understanding will guard your hearts and minds in Christ Jesus.* (Phil 4:6–7)

My home has truly been transformed into a safe haven. The pages that follow is the fruit of my time spent with the daily liturgical readings. I do not profess to write as a theologian, nor as a Scripture scholar; the words that follow are the product of biblical study, prayerful meditation, and, at times, spiritual imagination. May these reflections be a blessing to you as they have been a blessing to me. May God grant you the gift of discovering him in his word. And may he transform your home into a safe haven.

But in my quiet place with God I found rest, refuge; I understood the meaning of those verses, "Come to me all who are burdened, and I will give you rest" (Mt 11:28), and God is "my refuge and fortress" (Ps 91:2). I felt in that special place with him, my relationship with him cannot be penetrated by evil; it is a safe spot. Though evil may try to pull me away from my safe haven with him, when I am there, no evil can be there too. – Lindsey Leonard

ASH WEDNESDAY

(JL 2:12-18; PS 51:3-6, 12-14 AND 17; 2 COR 5:20-6:2; MT 6:1-6, 16-18)

And your Father who sees what is hidden will repay you.

Why does Jesus feel the need to repeat *three times* that God will "repay" us, as long as we keep our good works under wraps? Why is secrecy necessary in order to receive a "reward" for the good we do? Wouldn't it be of more benefit to people to witness our good example, that they might be inspired to follow it?

Well, let's understand what Jesus is saying here. He is not telling us to keep our "good example" a secret. Our good example should always shine forth like the sun, lighting the path for others, that they might find their way. What he is asking us to forgo is the seeking of *earthly* rewards for our acts of charity, which can so often be a temptation for those of us stiving for holiness.

Years ago, my parish was pretty big on giving away awards and accolades to people who helped out around the church. Every year twelve people were picked who exemplified outstanding service to the parish community. The idea was to show gratitude towards the ones who gave of themselves selflessly, and to encourage others to do the same. Of course, for the ones who wanted to simply serve the Lord, it was a little uncomfortable to stand up in front of the whole congregation to the sound of all that applause. But there was another insidious problem that started to creep in.

I remember the year that I was chosen for the award, a handful of people from the parish came up to congratulate me. But there was one woman in particular who said to me, "That's great that you won the award. Do you know I won that award as well a few years ago? And last year the diocese awarded me such and such, and my husband and I both won the award for this other such and such …" And herein lay the issue of what was troubling me about all the award giving at my parish. For most of us, winning things feels *good.* Really good! It encourages us to do more, to do better, to keep going. Certainly, there is nothing wrong with that. But pretty soon, we can find ourselves doing those good things for the sake of the reward, and not for the sake of pleasing God. When we do good for God alone, it should actually feel … *unrewarding.* Tithing, sweeping up other people's dirty tissues and goldfish crumbs left on the church floor after Mass, stapling thousands of newsletters, or chauffeuring senior citizens from their nursing homes to church on cold winter days should not feel "fun" to us. And if we do it because of how good we feel when others notice, then we risk losing the reward we could have received if God *alone* had noticed. But what reward could God possibly give us, if not to feel good when we're doing not-so-fun jobs? The gift of *humility.*

Now motherhood is about the best example of built-in humility that comes with the job. Why? Because *no one* rewards a mother for her sacrifice during those 3 AM nursing sessions, those endless cycle of toilets to be cleaned, laundry to be folded, dishes to be washed, meals to be prepared. Most of the time, her kids don't thank her for the folded socks. But if she misses a day of laundry, she will get a "Where are my socks??" And a grumpy teenager will show her impression of a meal by saying nothing ... unless there's not enough salt, or if the chicken is a little dry. In that case, that teenager will miraculously regain the ability to speak! A mother's work is *expected* of her, not repaid, and what's more, every other mother is in the same boat, so it's not like she's anything special just because she has a lot to do. She indeed gives good example for her family to see, and hopefully her children grow to follow her in virtue. But as she serves, it is nearly impossible to get an earthly reward for being a mother. *Thank God.*

And your Father who sees in secret will repay you.

There are few jobs more humbling and universally lacking in earthly reward than being a mother. But humility is not the *only* "recompense" God wishes to give us. This is the recompense for our "righteous deeds" that we do "in secret." What recompense does he give us for the other two acts of the will Jesus mentions in today's Gospel — specifically, prayer and fasting?

When Jesus tells us not to be "like the hypocrites, who love to stand and pray in the synagogues," of course he is not telling us to stop praying in church. He is telling us not to pray in church "*so that* others may see." In other words, our prayer should not be for the purpose of appearances, but for the purpose of uniting ourselves with him. That is why our predawn prayer hour fills us with such light! Absolutely nobody would know or care whether we got out of bed at 5 AM to pray; we are not doing it for anyone else. Our early morning prayer is solely for the sake of spending time with Jesus. But if Jesus still wants us to go to church to pray within a community, what will make that time of prayer not for the sake of appearances, but rather, for him alone? Perhaps he showed us the answer to that question at the beginning of the COVID-19 pandemic when churches first closed. That time of stillness, as isolating and lonely as it was for so many of us, was also an opportunity, like we'd never had before, to *reflect*. Deprived of his Eucharistic presence, the question that should have burned in our hearts in our deepest moments of silence was: "What are you doing in this, Lord?" In all the confusion, anger, anxiety, and division that engulfed our world … perhaps Jesus was teaching us what the prayer of our Church community was meant to be. When we pray in church, united with our brothers and sisters — especially in a time of collective suffering — we are united not because we all have the same opinions and agree on every matter, but rather, because we are united in *him*. In the *Eucharist*. Our Church prayer, then, is meant to unite us as one, while at the same time our prayer is in "secret," a joining of hearts between Jesus and ourselves. The period of time in which we watched Mass livestreamed seemed to be a shadow of our true worship … *except* for one thing: in a certain sense, *this was God's will for us*. World renowned public speaker Father Mike Schmitz was asked by many how it could be possible to be sustained in grace when we'd been deprived of daily Mass which had been our lifeline before. And his reply was,

"Because we priests are praying for *you*." Every time our priests received the Body and Blood of Christ, they received it on behalf of the whole Church. Our ardent, heartfelt, *yearning* spiritual Communion was united to their physical Communion, such that, "the effect of the sacrament [could] be secured by every person if he [received] it in desire, though not in reality" (St. Thomas Aquinas, *Summa Theologiae*, III). Can we even imagine the graces? Of course, nothing could "replace" the physical reception of Christ's Body and Blood in the Eucharist, which, Aquinas goes on to say, if received properly, "produces more fully the effect than does the desire thereof." But when physical Communion is not possible for us, Christ's reward when we hide ourselves in his cloak, *longing* for his shelter and refuge, is an abundance of grace. It is this "secret" prayer that Jesus asks of us, whether we are alone with him at 5am, or receiving him alongside an entire church full of people at Mass.

Finally, Jesus asks that when we fast, we "may not appear to be fasting." Well, I, for one, have never liked to fast. Typically, Ash Wednesday and Good Friday have been the days on the liturgical calendar that I have dreaded the most. As soon as I hit fifty-nine, I am old enough to be off the hook — right? The thing is, if that is my attitude, then I do not really understand the point of fasting. If that is my attitude, then I am fasting for *appearances*; that is, simply because the Church says so and I'm supposed to follow the rules. Perhaps that is a start … but if I keep it at a "start," then I've advanced no farther along spiritually than the eight-year-old child who dreads going to confession, repeating the same old list of "I hit my sister" and "I disobeyed my parents." The reality is, the power of fasting is *incredible*. It is *life changing*. It is *miraculous*. Offered with trust, fasting has the power to obtain for us the most profound desire of our hearts, hidden deep within. That "impossible" conversion we have been begging the Lord for? Let us fast. That healing? Let us fast. That broken heart? Let us fast. No, it is not a magic formula to get everything we want, but it is one of the most powerful tools God has given us to obtain everything we need. He has given us a way, handed on a silver platter! So why don't we use it, as the early Church *regularly* did? Frankly, because it is hard. It is much easier to come up with an excuse, to do some other form of penance, or to "just" pray because, after all, no one would even notice whether we're fasting or not. And herein lies the secret to fasting. When we willfully give up our legitimate need and desire — unseen by anyone else — God then "rewards" us by taking care of *everything.* When we fast, our prayer is answered almost before we've had the chance to ask. Now it is true, there will be times when we will ask for a healing and still, that one remains ill. But when we fast for that one, we can be sure that Jesus will heal them where they need it most. And thus, our fasting in secret will obtain for us the greatest grace we can have here on earth: the gift of peace ... in *all* things.

Behold, now is a very acceptable time; behold, now is the day of salvation.

THURSDAY AFTER ASH WEDNESDAY

(DT 30:15-20; PS 1:1-4, 6; LK 9:22-25)

I have set before you life and death, the blessing and the curse.

Why was it not obvious to the children of Israel that they should choose "life" and "blessing" over "death" and "the curse"? It wasn't like this was *Let's Make a Deal* where the contestants can't see what's behind curtain number one and curtain number two. There were no "lucky" guesses involved. God spelled out plainly what it would take to receive the blessing, and what it would take to receive the curse. All that was left for the Israelites to do was to *choose.*

Let's examine, then, what the conditions were for the two choices, and why the choice to be blessed wasn't such a no-brainer for the Israelites. These were the conditions the people would have to follow in order to receive the blessing and live:

1. *Love the Lord*
2. *Heed his voice*
3. *Hold fast to him*

And under what conditions would the Israelites receive the curse? If they:

1. *Turn away their hearts*

2. *Do not listen*
3. *Are led astray and adore and serve other gods*

So why did God have to warn them to "choose life" when it should have been obvious to them which choice to make, and he even spelled out thc precise steps it would take to receive the blessing? If I explain to my daughter how to make the perfect homemade chocolate cake, and then tell her that if she uses the box mix, she will be disappointed in the taste, I should not have to end with: "Choose homemade." It should be self-evident. But do you know what? She may just opt for the mix anyway. Now why would she do that if she has already been warned that her cake won't taste as good? Because she hears what I have said ... but she is not really listening. She's thought about it ... but then she looks at the recipe I've given her ... and then looks at the box. Sure, the box is not the real thing ... but do you know what that box offers her? It offers her an *easy* way. That box does not require a lot of effort, whereas my recipe calls for so many ingredients! She would have to go to the store to buy the things she doesn't have on hand. Not to mention all the work involved in buttering and flouring the pans, washing all those dishes afterwards ... by the time she gets it in the oven, it will be *hours* before she can enjoy a slice. That box mix, however, will be done in a jiffy. No patient waiting required at all, just good old-fashioned instant gratification! To her, my recipe makes no sense to invest in at all. Once she has laid out the pros and cons in her head, doing things the right way no longer seems like the better option. Yes, she has some vague notion of the disappointing results that will await her ... but that seems so far off in the future it hardly matters right now. She can worry about the consequences later. For now, she has convinced herself that the most satisfying option lies behind curtain number two.

Such was the disposition of the Israelites. Despite the admonitions, warnings, and recipe itself handed to them on a silver platter, when it came down to it, what was involved in choosing curtain number one was too much for them in their view. Curtain one would require *patience*, and after four hundred years of slavery, they were not too keen on the Lord's timetables when it came to waiting, eternally speaking. It would also require *trust*, something else they had failed to hold on to as a result of not seeing their prayers answered with the speed they would have liked. It's not that the ancient Israelites didn't have faith; their faith was the one thing they managed to pass on generation after generation, despite their enslavement. Their problem was not that they did not believe there was a God; their problem was that they stopped *trusting* he would take care of them. Deep down, they believed that if they did not take matters into their own hands, God was not going to do it for them either. Finally, to choose curtain number one would require "walking in his ways;" that is, continual self-sacrifice. The Jews had already endured so much *imposed* sacrifice by the Egyptians; the thought of voluntarily giving up even more of themselves must have been repugnant to them. So what did they do? They stopped listening to God's "advice." His advice was abhorrent, as far as they were concerned. His advice would subject them to a life of bitter misery, so they would have concluded. And when any of us stops listening to God, by definition, we stop loving him. Why? Because Jesus tells us:

If you love me, you will keep my commandments. (Jn 14:15)

Our love for God is not shown in sweet sentiments or lofty prayers, though these can certainly come pouring out of us as a natural consequence of our love for him. The only way we *prove* our love for God, however, is by being obedient to his word. Period.

So the Israelites stopped listening, and they stopped loving, two of the three conditions under which they would receive the curse of death. There was just one condition left, which, tragically, they did eventually meet: they were led astray.

When we stop listening to the voice of God, it's not like we remain neutral or in limbo until the time we decide to pick ourselves back up and listen to him again. Listening to God does not take evenings and weekends off. We do not get "vacations" from obedience. To not be obedient necessarily means that we choose to be *disobedient*. And if we choose not to listen to God, we will choose to listen to someone else. But let's understand: that other voice we listen to will not simply be someone's harmless "opinion;" it will be the voice of *deceit*. Jesus told John that "whoever is not against us is for us" (Mk 9:40), the implication being that the reverse is also true: whoever is not for Jesus is *against* him. We simply cannot listen to a voice that professes anything contrary to the teachings of God, voiced in the words of Scripture, and explained to us by the Church. It is true, those other voices can be quite compelling and convincing, and they certainly can give us pause to question and doubt. But let's then bring our questions to Jesus in prayer, the Sacraments, and the word, that he may *clarify* our understanding and strengthen our faith even more than before. Let's transform what the devil intends for evil into the good that God always wills for our lives.

Even though you meant harm to me, God meant it for good. (Gen 50:20)

So what does Jesus clarify for us today?

... whoever loses his life for my sake will save it.

"Walking in his ways" and "keeping his commandments" is not meant to be "quick" or "easy." So we have to stop expecting that which Jesus never promised. What did he promise us? *Joy.* And not just joy, but "complete" joy (Jn 15:11). But if that is the case, why does life feel so hard? Why am I not having more fun? Two points here. One, in the Christian life, "joy" does not translate into "fun." It does, however, translate into "peace that surpasses all understanding" (Phil 4:7). There is a calm demeanor to Christian joy, one that does not get overly excited when things go our way, nor does it fall into despair when things don't. There is a contentment within the soul of a Christian that no one can take away, and a Christian who experiences this kind of joy knows where to go when she needs her spiritual tank refilled during trying times: right back to the temple of her heart where Christ resides. Walking in his ways means that a Christian smiles — and laughs — *a lot!* She sees the hand of God in all her circumstances, even the most perplexing ones, and it is this eternal perspective that lifts her soul.

Secondly, to receive that kind of joy, we must *first* "walk in his ways;" that is, we must "deny [ourselves] and take up [our] cross daily and follow [him]." Admittedly, that part is not going to *feel* fun. But there is still a way to be filled with joy, not only after we have accomplished his will, but even *during* the trial. That way is by doing "*whatever* he tells [us]" (Jn 2:5). Um ... isn't that the same thing as picking up that miserable cross he's handed us? Not exactly. When Jesus hands us a cross, sometimes we reject it, but most of the time, for those of us sincerely striving for holiness, we do manage to pick it up. The problem is, that's not *all* we pick up. We pick up the cross Jesus has handed us ... plus a bunch of *extra* baggage. We pick up the weight of "what if this happens." We pick up "why is this happening to me." We pick up "maybe I should do something." We pick up "it's all up to me to fix it." And this is where our cross turns into a heavy burden, too much for us to carry. Jesus asks us to focus on today — even just this single moment — and do the *next thing.* Instead, our minds go to: "What if this gets worse one year from now?" If we truly focused on simply doing "whatever he tells [us]"— nothing less, but also, *nothing more* — then we will find the greatest gift Jesus intends for our lives on earth: the grace of peace in all things.

> *Choose life, then, that you and your descendants may live, by loving the LORD, your God, heeding his voice, and holding fast to him.*

FRIDAY AFTER ASH WEDNESDAY

(IS 58:1-9; PS 51:3-6, 18-19; MT 9:14-15)

This, rather, is the fasting that I wish: releasing those bound unjustly, untying the thongs of the yoke; Setting free the oppressed, breaking every yoke; Sharing your bread with the hungry, sheltering the oppressed and the homeless; Clothing the naked when you see them, and not turning your back on your own.

Well, that is a rather lengthy list of instructions to follow in order to fast the way God intends us to. All I did on Ash Wednesday was cut back on food and abstain from meat! Does my fast, then, not fulfill the obligation?

Of course, the Lord is not simply telling the Israelites to go grab a falafel and then split it with someone in prison. He is saying that to fast with the intention of obtaining God's graces, while acting like a hypocrite, "quarreling and fighting" with our neighbor, begets us no grace at all; therefore, we should not be surprised when we do not receive it. Grace does not come to us by following a prescribed set of rules; unless those rules are followed not just with our hands, but also with our hearts. That's because God communicates himself to us primarily by way of the heart, which manifests itself in the form of *peace*. Then, secondarily, he answers our temporal needs according to his will and what's best for us and others: he heals illness (or allows it to remain), he gives financial support (or permits the struggle), he finds us the job, the home, the spouse (or keeps them outside our reach). If our hearts sincerely seek him, he will grant us our hearts' desire, though what he brings us may not be the thing we were expecting. We may not get what we were hoping for, but he promises to bring us what we really need: rest in our union with him. Sometimes the best way to accomplish that end is through the things we want; sometimes the better way is through our suffering.

> "You are asking for something that would be harmful to your salvation if you had it— so by not getting what you've asked, you are really getting what you want." — St. Catherine of Siena

God wants a change of heart before we can expect him to answer our "cry for help." But if he just wants our "hearts," why does he list so many specific actions for us to follow in our fast? Why not just say, *Love Me*? Because love is not proven in feeling or sentiment, though feelings of love certainly make us feel good. When I was first dating my husband, I loved him so much I thought my heart would burst! It was so ... *exciting* to be around him, I felt like I was perpetually on cloud nine! I felt as though I would do anything for him; I would move to Antarctica if it meant I would not have to spend my life without him. Wow. How magnanimous of me. The thing is ... there are plenty of young couples who felt the same way I did at the beginning of their marriage ... and have since divorced. Butterflies in the pit of our stomachs is not enough to keep us in Antarctica when the going gets tough. Only *love* can. Therefore, the word "love," though defined by the Oxford dictionary as "an intense feeling of deep affection," in the Christian sense, is better defined as *sacrifice*. The only way we prove our love for each other is if we're willing to forgo our wants for the sake of our neighbor's needs. And the only way we have to prove our love for God is to love our neighbor as ourselves.

So let's see ... when I fast, I must "release ... set free ... share bread ... shelter ... clothe ..." That is a rather tall order for a stay-at-home mom. But God is not asking me to ditch my kids on Fridays so I can go picket outside my town's local correctional facility and demand the release of convicted criminals. What he is saying is that the fast that he requires of us, in order to hear our "cry for help," is one in which we practice *mercy*. Now, sure, we understand why the corporal works of mercy are important and nice and everything ... but why is that the *condition* required for God to hear us? Why can't we just kind of be neutral, go about our day, fasting and praying for the desires of our hearts? Why does God not "hear" that kind of cry? Because there is no such thing as "neutral" when it comes to the spiritual life. In the physical life, if I have a task to do, I can take a break, table it for now, and pick back up where I left off once I resume. But in the spiritual life, if I don't keep going, I will inevitably drift *backwards*, much like what would happen if I were to stop paddling a canoe upriver against the current. But why does it work that way in the spiritual life? Because if I do not actively work to help relieve my neighbor's suffering, by definition, their suffering will be prolonged. If I do not seek to reconcile with my neighbor, by definition, she and I remain unreconciled. And if I do not work on forgiving my neighbor, by definition, I hold onto to unforgiveness. To ask God, then, to forgive my sins when I am not actively seeking to forgive others their transgressions against me, is not only hypocritical, but also an impossible request. Why? Because God will "forgive us our trespasses *as* we forgive those who trespass against us."

> *If you forgive others their transgressions, your heavenly Father will forgive you. But if you do not forgive others, neither will your Father forgive your transgressions.* (Mt. 6:14-15)

Practicing the works of mercy as we fast is not just nice or something "extra" to do during Lent. It is *mandatory*. The salvation of our very souls is at stake. Friends, this is a *dire* message from the Lord today.

> *Thus says the Lord GOD: Cry out full-throated and unsparingly ... Tell my people their wickedness and ... their sins.*

The Lord's message today certainly is a wakeup call as we recall the people in our lives who we struggle not to resent. He is telling us to have mercy on them in no uncertain terms: "full-throated" and "unsparingly." His message shakes us to the core; after all, the reality is, we've experienced some very real wounds in our lives; forgiveness isn't so easy for us! But as always, Scripture ends its message for us with the most uplifting ray of hope we could possibly be offered:

> *My sacrifice, O God, is a contrite spirit; a heart contrite and humbled, O God, you will not spurn.*

In order for the Lord to "answer" us when we "cry out" to him, we don't *only* have to have managed to wipe away all vestiges of resentment from our hearts before he'll come to help us. We just have to *try. Thank God.* Because the reality is, forgiveness is *impossible* by our human strength alone; we *need* God to fill our hearts with his grace to come swooping in and take over, in order to do the forgiving for us. How's that for a paradox? What begets his grace is not only the actual accomplishment of forgiveness, but the recognition of our utter powerlessness to forgive. A "heart contrite and humbled" is what *melts* the heart of the Father, such that he can't help but pour out his sweet grace upon our own. "Yes, yes- I'm coming!!" the Lord cries out to us. And hidden in the cloak of Jesus, we can *trust* him — in *everything.*

> *Then your light shall break forth like the dawn, and your wound shall quickly be healed; Your vindication shall go before you, and the glory of the LORD shall be your rear guard. Then you shall call, and the LORD will answer, you shall cry for help, and he will say: Here I am!*

SATURDAY AFTER ASH WEDNESDAY

(IS 58:9-14; PS 86:1-6; LK 5:27-32)

I take no pleasure in the death of the wicked man, says the Lord, but rather in his conversion, that he may live. (Ez 33:11)

Jesus was just not the Messiah that the Israelites were expecting, even though every shocking and revolutionary detail about him was foretold by the prophets. The Jews would have been well versed in Scripture; how could they have missed so much? And today's readings point to yet another shocking prophecy about the Messiah, which should not have surprised them at all. If only they had read the Torah as it was meant to be read: not as a religious rule book on piety, but as a love letter from the Lord; then they would have understood. The Messiah's goal was not to save his chosen people by "destroying" those who did not follow the "rules." The Messiah's goal would be to win those very souls over to the Kingdom too.

We can be a little harsh in our judgment of those righteous, exclusive Jews, but the reality is, we are not so unlike them. Sure, we can give ourselves a pat on the back for the charity we show to the poor, the elderly, the homebound, or the ones who do not know Jesus. And indeed, that service requires of us our time, talent, and treasure; no doubt God is pleased with our efforts to strive to recognize the face of Jesus in theirs. But this really is not a fair comparison to what the Jews had to endure when Jesus came on the scene, for two reasons. One, while it is true, some ignored or misinterpreted so much of the prophecy clearly laid out for them in Scripture, nobody had ever *explained* it to them the way Jesus did. Jesus was the *first* Rabbi to teach them what "I desire mercy, not sacrifice" really meant.

I grew up with a thorough CCD education. I remember going to weekly religion classes year after year, homework assignments and all. I prepared for all the Sacraments with proper instruction in the faith, right up through Confirmation; my mother saw to that. But it was not until I was in my late twenties that I heard as if for the first time that as Catholics, we believe Christ is really and truly present in the Eucharist, Body, Blood, Soul, and Divinity. Now certainly that little tidbit must have been mentioned along the way in my religious formation, particularly the year I prepared for my first Communion. But clearly, nobody *explained* it to me. By the time I understood the teaching as an adult, it was as if I had heard the news for the *first* time. It was a shock.

For those of us who sincerely seek to pursue the things of God, we are quite used to the concept of Jesus seeking the lost. We are right there with him, we want to help, we want to evangelize and bring others into the fold along with him — especially when it comes to the people we love who are away from the Church! So we're not really in the same boat as some of those ancient Jews; we already get it, we've been taught this lesson on a number of occasions; we're on board. Accepting this "radical" teaching is not so hard for us, as it was for many of those who were hearing it for the first time. At least on this point, we cannot compare ourselves to them equally.

But there is a second reason the teaching of Jesus on the conversion of the lost was so hard for the Jews to accept. Jesus was not asking them to welcome into their fold simply the poor, the possessed, the leper, the widow, the orphan; that is, the people who made them feel uncomfortable and they would have preferred not to notice. To accept these people would have been hard enough for them, but at least they may have had at least a small measure of sympathy for their misfortune. But Jesus was asking his chosen ones to go a step beyond welcoming the downtrodden. He was asking them — no, *requiring* them — to welcome also those who had *sinned against them*! And now we begin to understand their reaction.

> *This saying is hard; who can accept it?* (Jn 6:60)

Volunteering at a soup kitchen and offering counsel to those in need are very good things to do. Too few people give of their time to the service of the afflicted, so if we are one of those who do, Jesus is pleased, no doubt. But there is also a certain reward involved for us personally in helping someone to see the light. It feels *good* to bring lost souls to the loving heart of Christ. But what about the souls who are lost ... that also happen to get under our skin? What about the souls who churn up within us resentments we'd rather not bring to the surface? The ones who tempt us to react with a bite as they poke at our old wounds? The ones whose very presence brings a cloud of gloom and anxiety that threatens to destroy our peace? How eager are we to welcome those people into our fold? Do we dream about them in heaven with us one day? Do we pray for them heartily, as if they were our very own child? The truth is, it is more likely our "prayer" for them is a petition to God, asking him to make them to go away! Jesus wasn't just asking the chosen to bring their lost loved ones back into the fold. He was asking them to welcome into their Church the ones that they would never choose to love.

> *"Repairer of the breach," they shall call you, "Restorer of ruined homesteads."*

What Jesus asked of his own people is no different than what he asks of us today. We just have to recognize who it is he is asking us to help convert. We are to be called "repairer of the breach" and "restorer of the homestead." There is not a single one of us whose family couldn't use some repairing, and whose homesteads couldn't use some restoring. It is *we* who are to repair. It's up to *us* to restore.

Now if that sounds like an impossible task ... well, it is. At least it would be, *if* the Lord did not outline for us exactly *how* we can manage to repair breaches and restore homesteads. So let's look at what the Lord requires of us so that — you guessed it — it will be *he* who will actually be the One to repair and to restore:

> *Remove from your midst oppression, false accusation and malicious speech.*

First, though we may *feel* irritated, envious, or resentful, let us *act* as though we're not. An act of the will is not the same as pretending, because while the former genuinely seeks to practice virtue in order to obtain the spiritual gifts, the latter is motivated by hypocrisy, cowardice, and fear of confrontation. Love is an act of the will before it is a feeling. Our job is to lift up our hand; it is up to Jesus to supply the feeling (Corrie Ten Boom).

> *... bestow your bread on the hungry and satisfy the afflicted ...*

Once we have managed to act *as though* we are not envious or resentful, then we must make the firm decision to do "whatever" it is Jesus tells us to do (Jn 2:5). Sometimes we are so irritated with the one who's hurt us, it seems the best we can do is leave the room to keep ourselves from spewing words we would later regret. That's a start ... but Jesus calls us to a bit more. So let's get out from the blanket we've been hiding under and go offer a cup of coffee to the one who triggers our old wounds.

> *.... hold back your foot on the sabbath from following your own pursuits on my holy day ... honor it by not following your ways, seeking your own interests.*

Any day of the week is a good day for us to forgo our own interests for the sake of another. No, Jesus is not asking us to be doormats to anyone ... But he does want us to understand the power of sacrifice. Each time we submit to his will by forgoing our own, we are given the grace to repair and restore the very breach that has caused us to suffer. If we cannot understand how that could be, let's at least understand that it is a *mystery*; that is, something our minds can't fully understand in this life. But let's also realize that not understanding is not an excuse for not accepting. The alternative is to endure the unnecessary suffering that comes with unacceptance, the kind that makes a difficult situation worse. Suffice it to say, when we offer our suffering to the

Lord, he uses our offering to repair breaches, restore homesteads, and fill us with his peace. In this way, the suffering that causes us pain will work against itself to bring about the conversions and healings we seek.

Even though you meant harm to me, God meant it for good. (Gen 50:20)

FIRST SUNDAY OF LENT

GN 2:7-9; 3:1-7; PS 51:3-6, 12-14, 17; ROM 5:12-19; MT 4:1-11 (YEAR A)
GN 9: 8-15; PS 25: 4-9; 1 PT 3: 18-22; MK 1: 12-15 (YEAR B)
DT 26: 4-10; PS 91:1-2, 10-15; ROM 10:8-13; LK 4:1-13 (YEAR C)

If you are the Son of God, command that these stones become loaves of bread.

If I were in standing in Jesus' shoes, and knew the depths of my divine power and authority, what would have been my reaction to the devil's provocation? *Turn these puny stones into bread? Are you kidding me?? I'll show you who's boss — I'll turn that whole mountain over there into bread!!*

But Jesus, who, let's remember, is hungry, does not let his hunger turn into "hanger," as I surely would. Instead, he calmly combats the devil's temptation with Scripture. And not just any verse from Scripture, but the very verse that explains how he could possibly withstand fasting for forty days straight: Jesus "does not live on bread alone." His "food is to do the will of the one who sent [him]" (Jn 4:34). So the first thing Jesus reminds us when faced with temptation to sin is that it's not about this life, but the next.

If you are the Son of God, throw yourself down. For it is written: he will command his angels concerning you and with their hands they will support you, lest you dash your foot against a stone.

Then the devil, in his cunning, quotes Scripture right back to Jesus to "prove" his argument. Satan exhibits the epitome of misinterpreting Scripture out of context. Quoting Scripture out of context is a brilliant plan because, generally, it does succeed in confusing us. It gets us to think, "Wait — that does seem wrong ..." But while these confusing "proofs" can cause us to doubt, they do not pose a problem for Jesus at all. He already has perfect clarity in all the devil's misinterpretations and is therefore able to respond with an immediate:

You shall not put the Lord, your God, to the test.

The thing is ... couldn't Jesus have come up with a better Scripture passage to counter this second temptation the devil proposes regarding his command of the angels? Why not simply tell Satan, as he would say to his disciples later, "Do you think that I cannot call upon my Father and he will not provide me at this moment with more than twelve legions of angels?" (Mt 26:53). The reality is, when Jesus quotes the passage that said, "You shall not put your Lord God to the test," he is not saying, "The reason I'm not calling upon angels is because I don't want to test God." Rather, Jesus is essentially saying, "I'm not responding to your question because you are testing God." Just like the Pharisees, Satan was not interested in sitting at the feet of Jesus to seek understanding of the Scriptures.

When it comes to those who do not understand our faith, like Jesus, we too must distinguish between those who would engage in conversation with us in order to prove us wrong, and those whose hearts are open, sincerely seeking deeper knowledge of the divine. We do not have to avoid people who don't understand our faith simply because it's stressful to get into conversations with them. Maybe we're not so well versed in Scripture ourselves, let alone catechesis. But that's okay. Because if others come with open hearts, then we simply must place our focus on loving them; that much we can do. We do not have to worry about finding the perfect words to explain the faith because we "will be given at that moment what [we] are to say. For it will not be [we] who speak but the Spirit of [our] Father speaking through [us]" (Mt 10:19-20).

Now this is a great plan for those who come to us, ready to engage in discussion, with open hearts. But this was certainly not the disposition of Satan as he tempted Jesus in the desert, and, unfortunately, it is not the disposition of many in our world who have decided that moral good is relative. When such a person engages in conversation with us, it is not with an open heart, but rather, a disposition that seeks to prove us wrong. That is, they seek to "test" God (whether or not they perceive it that way). What is our response to be then? I know what our response sure wants to be: argument. Nothing gets under our skin more than someone attacking our faith, no matter how disguised that attack is in "harmless" opinion. Why shouldn't we argue? Why not stand up and defend our faith? Doesn't the alternative — remaining silent — give the appearance that we agree with their moral relativism?

The problem with "arguing" is that arguments do not tend to stay in the realm of its primary definition, which is: "a coherent series of reasons, statements, or facts intended to support or establish a point of view" (Merriam-Webster Dictionary). When we argue, we quickly devolve from "coherent" and "reasoned" to angry and hostile. It is this destructive arguing that is the ultimate goal of the evil one: if he can get Jesus to lose his peace and succumb to the temptation against charity, that's all he would need in order to "win." So how does Jesus respond? He simply points out Satan's ulterior motive, brings it to the light, and does not worry about whether he gets his point across or proves that he's right. Now, that is all well and good for conversations with the devil ... but not everyone who comes to us with a closed mind and heart is made up of pure evil. Some of those people are souls we love and care about very much! How do we remain uncaring about whether they have heard our message or not? While it is true that Jesus would have obeyed the Father's will with detachment, there is nothing uncaring about him at all. Jesus is the very heart of love and mercy itself! No one is more sorrowful when a soul turns away from him than he. Let's remember, when Peter denied Jesus three times, the Savior "turned and looked" at him (Lk 22:61), and he said nothing. But it is certain Jesus's heart was breaking. What do we suppose Jesus did next as he struggled to carry his cross to Calvary? Did he write Peter off? Did he think, *I'm done with him! I tried everything but Peter won't listen; he'll never change. It's hopeless.* No. Jesus would have *prayed* for Peter, by offering the very suffering his denial would have caused him, that it might work against itself, for the intention of Peter's conversion. And do you know what? It worked!

Recently, my husband and I sat down to watch a crime scene investigation show. In this particular episode, one of the investigators was going through a separation from his wife. He said to the main character, "You know, I know everything's going to be okay between us in the end." And the main character responded, "Yeah, I know. It's the middle part that's hard."

Friends, if we are in the "middle part," let's not lose hope or despair because we've already tried "everything." This is the time Jesus calls us to pray. But not "just" pray, the way we do when we rattle off novenas or make our rosaries a part of our routine. Not to dismiss those prayers; our faith tells us we can firmly believe in the power of just a single Hail Mary! It's just that, for those in need of conversion of heart, as Jesus told his disciples when they were unable to cast out the demon from the young man, "This kind can only come out through prayer" (Mk 9:8). Certainly, the disciples would have been praying … so what kind of prayer would Jesus have been referring to? The kind that holds on to trust, the kind that hopes against hope, the kind that has faith, despite the evidence to the contrary. It was hard for the disciples, no doubt. When their prayers were not "working," their faith that their prayers would ever work at all began to diminish. But Jesus was teaching them that this was the time to *increase* their trust, not abandon it. And yet ... it is one thing for Jesus, King of the Universe, to do such a thing; but how do souls as weak and little as we increase our faith amid circumstances that appear to be going from bad to worse? Fortunately, Jesus knows our weakness, and he loves us for it. He simply asks us to make an *act* of trust, whether or not we feel trustful. We leave it up to Jesus to supply the feeling. What does an act of trust look like? We cannot hear it enough: our trust is made manifest every time we offer Jesus a sacrifice of praise and thanks, sweating through it if we have to. That is how Jesus will increase our faith. Part two, of course, is that we pray for the faith of the one whose heart has been hardened by moral relativism. True, we are powerless to get inside someone else's heart and fix what has been wounded. But there is Someone who can: Our Lord and Savior Jesus Christ. If we want him to fix what is broken in the heart of another on our behalf, then we must simply unite our cross to his. That way, our problem becomes his problem. So how exactly do we unite our crosses to that of Jesus? By accepting the pinpricks, the inconveniences, the trials, and — most especially — the very suffering those in need of conversion have caused us, and offering it back to the Lord with all the love we can muster. If we still doubt it can work that way ... one look at how Peter turned out will prove to us that it is true.

All these I shall give to you, if you will prostrate yourself and worship me.

Finally, Satan hands Jesus one final attempt to bring him down. It's futile, and it's ridiculous, because how can anyone offer the King of the Universe a parcel of land on earth and think that's a temptation? At this point, if Jesus weren't so aggravated — and hungry — he would have laughed. But what does Jesus say to him instead?

Get away, Satan!

Jesus has finally cast him out. But that leaves us with one final question. Why didn't Jesus just tell the devil to "get away" right from the start? Why engage in all this back and forth when he could have gone home a long time ago?

My food is to do the will of the one who sent me.

It was the Father's will that Jesus should be tempted. He "was led by the Spirit into the desert to be tempted by the devil." Let's chew on that for a moment because often, especially for parents, our every instinct is to protect those we love from evil. And it is indeed a good and holy desire, one which the Father places on every parent's heart. But those ones we love — like us — must "work out their salvation with fear and trembling" (Phil 2:12), and that can only happen by way of temptation. Admittedly, it is hard to see our loved ones succumb to temptation — especially when the end is not in sight. The middle of the story is no fun. But. Let's look back at the "workout" we ourselves had to undergo in our own lives in order to get to where we are now. Oh, the mistakes.

Oh, the foolishness. Oh, the years spent in blindness, and then later, bitter regret. But now ... would we really change a thing? Without the mess we made of our lives, surely, we would not know the God of mercy that we know now. So let's trust that this same Heart of Mercy is working in the lives of our loved ones too. Our God of mercy would never allow the temptations in their lives unless he intended to draw good out of them. But that good will only come about if someone is praying for them … which we are. So let's take the courage Jesus offers us, and not lose heart. Jesus has a plan for the salvation of our loved ones. We just have not come to the last chapter; the best is yet to come.

> *For I know well the plans I have in mind for you ... plans for your welfare and not for woe, so as to give you a future of hope …* (Jer 29:11)

MONDAY OF THE FIRST WEEK OF LENT

(LV 19:1-2, 11-18; PS 19:8-10, 15; MT 25:31-46)

He will place the sheep on his right and the goats on his left.

There goes Jesus again with his first century Jewish analogies. For those of us who have only ever seen sheep at a petting zoo, we've had to be taught why Jesus took such a fancy to those furry friends of his. Sheep are docile, sheep follow their shepherd's voice, and sheep will give you the coats off their backs (quite literally). But still, for us modern-day Christians, it would just be easier for us to wrap our minds around the analogy if Jesus had said something like, "Golden retrievers on my right, crocodiles on my left." That, we would get. Golden retrievers are sweet, loyal, friendly, and trustworthy; crocodiles will eat you for lunch.

The thing is, I think golden retrievers are adorable, just as much as the next guy, but frankly, they don't put a lot of *thought* into obeying their master. They have the same innate trust that a baby has towards his mother. It is just what golden retrievers do, and it is one of the things we find so lovable about them. But it is kind of hard to aspire to be like a golden retriever, because unlike them, *we* mess up. We don't always follow our Master's directions without fail. The reality is, we are more like a sheep, who, though he knows what's best for him is to follow his shepherd's voice, still manages to occasionally get lost. What's more, we'd *rather* be in the position of sheep than we would golden retriever, because as sheep, our

Shepherd will come to find us if we've lost our way. All we have to do is bleat.

Now we look to the goats. Ok, we understand now why the sheep analogy makes more sense than that of golden retriever ... but what act of aggression did goats ever inflict upon anyone? The crocodile analogy makes a lot more sense! So why didn't Jesus use the crocodile analogy? Because just as the ones on his right did not get there because they were cute and friendly, neither did the ones on his left get there because they were dangerous and aggressive. There is only *one thing* that separates the right from the left:

> *Not everyone who says to me, "Lord, Lord," will enter the Kingdom of heaven, but only the one who does the will of my Father in heaven …* (Mt 7:21)

Jesus is not trying to teach us today that bad guys go to hell. Everyone *knows* where an unrepentant serial killer will end up. What he's trying to teach us is that those types of people are not the *only* ones who will end up on his left. There is a whole other category of people who are headed there but don't realize it, and Jesus want us to open our eyes lest we end up in that category ourselves.

So why goats? Those furry animals are about as appealing as sheep; what is so offensive about their behavior that they merit a spot at Jesus's left? The thing about goats is that they are not particularly docile, and definitely not so good at listening to their master's voice. Goats are *stubborn.* They prefer their own will to anyone else's, at all times. They are not necessarily doing anything "bad" — like the extreme violence of the crocodile who mauls an unsuspecting victim — it's just that, they don't do what they're *supposed* to be doing. And when that happens, others get hurt.

> *Then they will answer and say, "Lord, when did we see you hungry or thirsty or a stranger or naked or ill or in prison, and not minister to your needs?"*

The goats don't realize (or perhaps don't care) that every time they go off and do their own thing, in their own way, someone else has to suffer for it. No man is an island, and no action we commit involves just ourselves. Ever. We must realize that every decision we make will affect the whole body of Christ — for better or for worse — even when we think our act is hidden or isolated. Now maybe we cannot see how that can be. How can what I do with my own personal life affect you? It is indeed a mystery.

> *If [one] part suffers, all the parts suffer with it; if one part is honored, all the parts share its joy* … (1 Cor 12:26)

Suffice it to say, we cannot extend our vision so far that it reaches to all the ends of the earth; we cannot extend it back in time to the beginning, nor forward in time to the end. But there is Someone who can: Our Good Shepherd. That is why as his sheep, we must listen to his voice at all times, and follow it. If we do just that, we will be counted among the ones on his right.

Now of course, we don't always listen, and we don't always follow. Sometimes our actions *do* cause others to suffer as a consequence of our own stubborn self-will. What's a soul as weak and sinful as ourselves to do? Mercifully, St. Therese of Lisieux tells us that even if we were to have "on [our] conscience all the sins that can be committed," Jesus will forgive us… *if* we entrust ourselves to his mercy, with contrite hearts. Without this single act of humility, we will end up on Jesus's left. Jesus warns us of this today so that, unlike the goats, we will not be taken by surprise. It is blind pride that will cause us to blaspheme against the Holy Spirit, and frighteningly, if we do not heed Jesus's warning, we won't even recognize that we've done it.

Which leaves us with one final question. Did the sheep not ask almost the identical question as the goats?

> *Then the righteous will answer him and say, 'Lord, when did we see you hungry and feed you, or thirsty and give you drink? When did we see you a stranger and welcome you, or naked and clothe you? When did we see you ill or in prison, and visit you?"*

So what makes the goats "blind" and the sheep "righteous," if neither could see the consequence and value of their actions?

Because in the case of the goats, their pride blinded them to the hypocrisy of their sin, whereas in the case of the sheep, their *humility* shielded their own holiness from their personal view. The goats focused on themselves; the sheep focused on the all-encompassing love and mercy of God.

TUESDAY OF THE FIRST WEEK OF LENT

(IS 55:10-11; PA 34:4-7, 16-19; MT 6:7-15)

This is how you are to pray: ... Thy will be done...

One year in February, we had a warm front push in through the greater Buffalo area. Sunny skies and mild temperatures afforded us lots of time spent outdoors, enjoying a taste of spring. In fact, I had convinced myself that spring had indeed come early to Western New York. Ahhh. It felt so good to be done with winter.

Then came March, the month that officially ushers in the season of spring. Guess what came back to our neck of the woods with a vengeance? Snow, wind, and cloudy skies. In fact, it all started with an ice storm the likes of which I had never seen. My entire yard was one giant hockey rink. The kids had the week off from school, so they grabbed their helmets and their sleds and had a blast. I, however, did not dare leave the house for fear of slipping on the ice and breaking a much-needed body part. So instead, I looked out the window, and just like the Grinch who stole Christmas, I *complained.*

Now it is true, some of us are just a little more thin-blooded than others; for us, the cold really does seem to reach a little more to the core. But the thing about complaint is that it tends to make our hearts "two sizes too small." When we complain, it takes away our ability to see. To see what precisely? The hand of God in our circumstances. I called a friend to let her know what I thought of this weather, and you know what her response was? "I think it's pretty." *Pretty*?? What part of cold and cloudy in March is pretty? Well, if I had taken off my complaint glasses and put on her glasses of gratitude, I might have seen for myself.

> *... from the heavens the rain and snow come down and do not return there till they have watered the earth, making it fertile and fruitful, Giving seed to the one who sows and bread to the one who eats ...*

When the Lord sends us "rain and snow" (or anything else we find unpleasant), his intention is to make us "fertile and fruitful." When we accept whatever he sends with gratitude, we become like "the one who sows" and "the one who eats." In other words, God will send us his gifts, but they will do nothing for us unless we receive them with a thankful heart. My kids could have joined me on the couch lamenting, "I wish the sun would come back out so we could go outside and not just sit here." But then, they would never have created the unprecedented memory of launching down the most fantastic ice hill they'd ever sled. It was the thrill of a lifetime for them, one they will always remember with glee. I, on the other hand, will not particularly take note of the couch upon which I sat.

So right then and there I began to pray, "I'm sorry for complaining, Lord," and then, "Thank you for the cold and snow." And the result was immediate: right away I was given to understand the "seed" and "bread" that God had given me. If it had been warm and sunny that week as it had been the week before, there is no way I would have "wasted" my days inside. I would have certainly taken the kids to the playground, gone on lots of walks, enjoyed the fresh air ... and the indoor tasks I had needed to fulfill would have fallen by the wayside. Perhaps that doesn't sound like much to be grateful for, but in that time of prayer alone with the Lord, my eyes were opened to see it as a giant gift. What's more ... I did not have to go outside. I could look out the window to watch the kids have fun from the comfort of a warm blanket, a crackling fire, and a steaming cup of coffee. God let me borrow the gratitude glasses my friend had been wearing and now I could see just what she found so "pretty" about the cold.

So shall my word be that goes forth from my mouth; It shall not return to me void, but shall do my will, achieving the end for which I sent it.

Now the thing about not accepting the gifts that God sends us is that we tend to think if we complain, he'll just give up on us and leave. Isn't that what St. Faustina tells us about grace? That if we reject it, Jesus will give it to someone else? The thing is, there is a difference between "not accepting" and "rejecting." If it sounds like semantics, it's really not. There are some circumstances in life that are exceedingly difficult to accept: the loss of a loved one ... the diagnosis of a serious illness ... a global pandemic. The Lord knows we are not impervious to pain; our hearts are not made of stone, but flesh, and so acceptance does not always come immediately for us. On the days that it does, it is his grace granting us a “freebie.” But on the days that it does not, the Lord is patient, kind and merciful. He understands. He can wait. And he will not allow his grace to "return to [him] void, but shall do [his] will, achieving the end for which [he] sent it." His word shall not return to him until we, who sincerely desire to accept his will, but just *can't* right now, finally do come to accept it. But what does that mean? That as soon as we accept, he leaves us? Of course not. It simply means that during the times in which we are struggling — that is, the "middle part" of our trial — it is then that Jesus carries us through.

The LORD is close to the brokenhearted; and those who are crushed in spirit he saves.

One we have accepted our trial, the grace we receive is the gift of peace in all things. His grace remains, taking over our hearts as a reward for our struggle to practice the virtue of gratitude in the darkness when we could not see. We persevere in offering again and again a "sacrifice of praise," and in exchange, the Lord sees to it that our praise no longer feels like "sacrifice" at all, but rather, as genuine and natural to us as breathing. The grace that remains is that we are truly peaceful and full of joy, even though the trial itself may not yet have come to an end.

So we understand how God's word remains with us and does not return to him void when we've struggled to accept ... but how is this any different for the ones who reject the graces God sends?

The difference is this: a soul who rejects God's grace does not want to accept it. It's not just that they can't; it's that they *won't.* Now before we go thinking, "Who would ever willingly choose to reject grace," let's realize that at times, that person has been *us*. Anytime we do not look for the hand of God in our circumstances, anytime we think it's not "supposed" to be this way, any time we believe that what is happening to us is somehow outside of God's purview … it's a temptation to reject the graces he intends for us. And when we do that, we end up stuck in bitter, sterile complaint, void of peace and void of joy.

One does not live on bread alone, but on every word that comes forth from the mouth of God. (Mt 4:4)

Accepting our circumstances as from the hand of God — whether by way of his ordained will or his permissive will — does not mean we won't experience sorrow in them, and so we should not expect that. Sorrow too is a gift from God that breaks open our hearts in a capacity to love like nothing else. What acceptance does for us is to allow the peace of Christ to come ushering in, such that it might coexist right alongside our sorrow. Without that peace, our trials become unbearable. But with it, that which we must endure becomes bittersweet. Bitter, because it still causes us pain; but also sweet, because we now see the good that God has drawn out of our trial. So much so, that we can honestly say we wouldn't change our circumstances if we could. God has already changed our hearts.

Your Father knows what you need before you ask him.

WEDNESDAY OF THE FIRST WEEK OF LENT

(JON 3:1-10; PS 51:3-4, 12-13, 18-19; LK 11:29-32)

My sacrifice, O God, is a contrite spirit; a heart contrite and humbled, O God, you will not spurn.

Yesterday's readings reminded us that if we are struggling to accept a difficult circumstance in our lives, the most efficacious way to receive God's light is to offer him a sacrifice of praise and thanks. But today, we discover, there is a second kind of sacrifice that is pleasing to God, one that, just like praise and thanks, does not involve goats or lambs or any blood at all, and yet "pays" the price we owe God for our sins. Goodness ... what payment could that possibly be? Is it the sackcloth and ashes that the Ninevites wore in today's first reading? That seemed to do the trick; God then "repented of the evil that he had threatened to do to them." Or perhaps it was the fasting? Is this the "sacrifice" we must perform to make up for all those memories of our past shameful behavior that still make us cringe? What about hanging on to guilt — will this do it? Not forgiving ourselves? Carrying around the heavy burden of belief that we are undeserving of God's love?

Of course, we would tell anyone else that if they believe those things about the "price" of sin, then they really do not know God. And yet, we believe those things ourselves, even if rather subconsciously and to a lesser degree than we did in the past. No, it should be obvious to us by now, even though it may be hard to believe, that God requires just one sacrifice to "make up" for our sin: we need only be "contrite and humble" of heart.

Now we know this ... in theory. But in practice ... it just does not seem right. It seems too easy. After all, in the criminal justice system, a judge doesn't allow a thief or a murderer to get away with his crime scot-free simply for mumbling an apathetic "Sorry." The judge does not respond "That's okay," and then let the criminal go his merry way. That criminal must receive a punishment for his crime, in order to satisfy the debt he owes to the one whose rights he has violated. So why does God so easily say "That's okay" to us when we say we are sorry? Well, he doesn't. For one thing, forgiveness of sins is not the same as saying "That's okay." Sin is not okay, under any circumstances, so when God forgives us, that is not what he's telling us. Forgiveness says, "I won't hold this offense against you." So in the criminal case, even if the judge were to say "That's okay," it's not up to him to forgive the offense. It is up to the one who was offended. Therefore, for us, the reason we forgive those who offend us is so that we ourselves are set free. It is so that their offense no longer has a hold on us. And so that God, in turn, will forgive us our own transgressions.

So if God doesn't say "That's okay" when we say "I'm sorry" ... what does he say? He says, "I've erased your sin from my memory." So why do we hold onto it in ours? Because to be forgiven, we can't only say we're sorry. What else must we do? Is this where the ashes, sackcloth and fasting come in? No. The Psalms tell us that a heart "contrite and humble God will not spurn." In other words, if we are having trouble forgiving ourselves ... if we are having trouble believing that God really does forgive us ... if we are having trouble letting go of our sinful past even though we are truly sorry ... then it is because we haven't met the second requirement to forgiveness: humility of heart. But how is it possible that we are not humble when we feel so bad about ourselves? Because humility has nothing to do with feeling "bad;" rather, it is a disposition of the *heart.* Humility is neither shocked at the realization of the sin we are capable of, nor does it allow us to think "I would never" when we witness the sinful actions of others. Humility brings to mind all the times we've acted in the very same sinful way as they. Humility causes us to realize that if we have not fallen into one sin or another, it is 100% due to the grace of God preserving us, because without that grace, we surely could. Humility does not allow us to judge our neighbor, pointing out to us that we have no way of knowing every factor in other people's lives that has led them to commit the sins they do. Humility prevents us from expecting that we are never going to fall again in the future, but it also leads us to trust with all confidence in the mercy of God.

It is no wonder that humility is the agent of peaceful acceptance. It doesn't make us forget our past (after all, it's good to remember what we are capable of), but it does enable us to let it go.

God repented of the evil he threatened to carry out on the people of Nineveh, not because of all the ashes and sackcloth and fasting, but rather because they "turned from [their] evil way." It was their humble contrition that melted his heart, not their physical acts of penance in reparation for their sins. Which leaves us with the question: why bother with the other kinds of sacrifices at all, if the only ones God requires are praise and thanks and humble contrition? We bother with those other sacrifices because of what those spiritual disciplines do for *us*. Fasting is not "payment" for our sins, just as it wasn't for Jesus when he was led by the Spirit to be tempted in the desert. Fasting strengthens us, so that we might grow to detach from the sins that have a hold on us, and it prepares us for what lies ahead. So too when we "offer up" our irritations, our inconveniences, or even our much heavier trials, we unite our cross to that of Jesus, that he may bring grace to the lives of others … which fulfills the deepest desire of our hearts. That is how we obtain miracles and healings and conversions. Those kinds of sacrifices do not "buy" forgiveness; besides which, any punishment we inflict upon ourselves could never amount to the punishment we deserve. Jesus already paid that price. The point of our discipline, then, is to keep our hearts humble and contrite, and to obtain that same humility of heart in the lives of those for whom we pray. And for that, we would do anything.

> *Even now, says the LORD, return to me with your whole heart for I am gracious and merciful …* (Jl 2:12-13)

One last note about our penances. While they do not "pay" for our sins, amazingly, they do offer reparation. It is like the young boy who breaks his mother's favorite mug, and then tries to make up for it as best he can by gluing the handle back on. That mom could have fixed it herself (with better aptitude and competence), but she gives her son the opportunity to try to fix it anyway — not so much for her benefit, but for his. Though a scar remains … love makes it good as new.

THURSDAY OF THE FIRST WEEK OF LENT

(EST C:12, 14-16, 23-25; PS 138:1-3, 7-8; MT 7:7-12)

Do to others whatever you would have them do to you.

Isn't this a strange way for Jesus to end his teaching on *ask, seek, knock*? After all, being nice to our neighbor is a good thing for us to do, of course ... but what does that have to do with asking Jesus for a personal need? It would seem to make more sense if Jesus were to have concluded his teaching with something such as, "And so the moral of the story is, the more you trust, the more I will fulfill the desires of your heart. The End." But no, Jesus doesn't end this way. He essentially ends with, "Put yourself in your neighbor's shoes and then treat him like that." So why would Jesus lump together two seemingly disconnected thoughts? He would not. That is to say, if they *seem* disconnected to us, it is simply because we haven't grasped the connection. Therefore, the only conclusion we are left with is that the Father's answering our prayers is *dependent* upon whether we treat our neighbor as we ourselves would like to be treated. In the same way that God will forgive us any sin ..."*as* we forgive those who trespass against us." But wait a minute. Didn't we learn yesterday that a humble, contrite heart is what it takes to be forgiven? And doesn't St. Faustina tell us that it is the prayer of one who *trusts* that "forces" Jesus to grant great graces? Yes, and yes. But today, Jesus expands on what it means to be humble and what it means to trust.

Very often, when something weighs heavily on our hearts, we are "seized with the mortal anguish" of Esther and can find it very difficult to pray as we normally do, let alone pray with greater trust. What seizes us the most is the uncertain "what if's" of the future. And in those moments, we tend to have trouble concentrating on anything else but our worries. We mistakenly believe that if we are not focused on how awful our problem is, or what consequences it could mean for the future, then we have stopped praying, we have stopped tallying up the persistence tokens God requires in order to fulfill the prescription we need. But this is not what Jesus means by "ask and you shall receive," nor is this what "pray without ceasing" looks like. When Jesus tells us that we "shall" receive when we ask, then that means we *shall* receive. As in, *will* receive. That "will" might come pretty quickly, but on the other hand, for God "one day is like a thousand years" (2 Pet 3:8) ... and so if we lose heart after day one, our faith isn't going to last very long (think here of the 400 years the ancient Israelites had to wait to be set free from slavery). So what does Jesus expect us to do while we're waiting? Twiddle our thumbs? Grouch at our spouse and kids because we're stressed out? Go hide under a blanket as we wait for someone to wake us up when it's all over? No. Jesus tells us exactly what we are supposed to do:

Do to others whatever you would have them do to you.

In other words, we do the next thing, according to our state in life and as prompted by the Holy Spirit. We do not neglect our good deeds simply because we're worried about something really big and really dire. Doing good to others does not mean we deny the gravity of our problems. It's just that focusing on the seriousness of our difficulties does nothing to solve them, and in fact, will tend to do the opposite. It will *increase* our anxiety and fear, which is precisely the disposition that prevents us from discerning God's will, the only thing that will work towards finding an *actual* solution to our difficulties. Doing the good to others that God calls us to will keep us rooted in his will, and says, "Lord, I'll do what little I can do according to your will. But as for the impossibility of the rest, I entrust that to you."

Help me, who am alone and have no help but you ...

Ok, this makes sense. We want to remain in God's will always; we long for that disposition of heart that truly responds in peaceful surrender. And yet, if we are so busy doing good to others, isn't that just another way of ignoring our much bigger problem? Isn't this simply the Christian method of putting a blanket over our heads and pretending everything is fine? Shouldn't we spend more time praying "without ceasing," as St. Paul advises?

Most certainly we are called to pray without ceasing. But not necessarily the way Queen Esther did, who "lay prostrate upon the ground ... from morning until evening." (I don't know about you, but as for me, I couldn't do that and get my laundry folded at the same time.) There is most definitely a place for prostrate prayer, but this is not the "unceasing" prayer that St. Paul refers to. So, what is he referring to? Let's see what he says next to find out:

> *In all circumstances give thanks, for this is the will of God for you in Christ Jesus …* (1 Thess 5:18)

Oh. My. Goodness. If we want to receive when we ask, then the way to pray unceasingly for the desire of our hearts is to *thank* God for the very circumstance that causes us pain. It is incredibly simple ... but also, incredibly counterintuitive. Who would ever say "thank you" for a stone or a snake? Only the one who has eyes to see the loaf of bread hidden in that stone, and the one who trusts a fish is soon on the way. That is why "thank you" is code for "I trust you" in the spiritual life. That is why praise and thanks beget us the grace we seek. And it is precisely why Queen Esther, who was "seized with mortal anguish," began her prayer in precisely this way:

> *[She] said: "God of Abraham, God of Isaac, and God of Jacob, blessed are you."*

Friends, if we are experiencing the "mortal anguish" of Esther in our own lives right now, the best way to receive the resolution we ask for is to *thank* God for the very thing that causes us pain. We'll only be able to do that if we recognize that it is God who sent it — whether by way of his ordained will or his permissive will — "for [our] welfare and not for woe" (Jer 29:11). And if we need a little help understanding "how can this be," (Lk 1:34), there is nothing wrong with asking the Lord to show us his hand in our circumstances. Such a prayer doesn't "test" God at all. It is the prayer of a little one who is weak and struggling and is sincerely trying to trust ... and wants more than anything to become a saint. It is the kind of prayer that *melts* the tender heart of Mercy. Finally, let's focus on doing the next thing. Placing our focus on God's will does not mean we have forgotten we have a problem. Jesus has not forgotten it either. He is busy ... taking care of *everything*.

When I called, you answered me; you built up strength within me.

FRIDAY OF THE FIRST WEEK OF LENT

(EZ 18:21-28; PS 130:1-8; MT 5:20-26)

When someone virtuous turns away from virtue to commit iniquity, and dies, it is because of the iniquity he committed that he must die.

Well, that is frightening. Not so much for those of us sincerely desiring to follow Christ and striving to live the holy life; sure, we fall, but we know enough to bring ourselves to the throne of mercy and pick ourselves back up and try again. No, the fear isn't so much for ourselves. But most of us have loved ones that used to be on board with the teachings of the Church, but now find those teachings do not match their wants. They have traded what *is* right for what feels right. That's not to say they don't have reason to: a culture that screams the "religion" of relativism; a clergy scandal that has let us down; the examples from the very people in the pews — some who are apathetic about the faith, picking and choosing which beliefs they will adhere to, while others who claim to be faithful act like hypocrites. We can certainly understand the cause of confusion among those who have turned away. And yet, the Lord is pretty clear today: if we turn away from virtue, we will be veering off the narrow path that leads to life (Mt 7:14).

You say, "The LORD's way is not fair!" Hear now, house of Israel: Is it my way that is unfair, or rather, are not your ways unfair?

Honestly, God's admonition does seem a little "unfair." His

words of warning seem to be the words of an exacting judge, not those of a merciful father. These words could be construed as fuel for those faithful "hypocrites" to promote their cause of finger-pointing and judgment. Except for one thing: the Lord tells us it does not have to be this way.

> *... if the wicked, turning from the wickedness he has committed, does what is right and just, he shall preserve his life; since he has turned away from all the sins that he committed, he shall surely live ...*

The ones we love are not doomed to continue on the broad path that leads to destruction if they do but one thing: *turn back*. So this sobering tale is in reality a lesson in *mercy*. Months ... years ... *decades* spent steeped and enmeshed in sin, can be wiped away with one single act of repentance, such that "none of the crimes he committed shall be remembered against him." That is mercy beyond comprehension. When someone has betrayed us — and especially when that betrayal has been serious and over the course of a long period of time — we might eventually come to the point of forgiving that one, though it would be exceedingly difficult for us. But even with that act of release from the resentment we had been holding onto, we do not simply "forget" the betrayal. We do not trust the offender as we did before because, quite frankly, that would be imprudent. And though we sincerely may have love for them in our hearts, we may not allow them into our lives the way we did before because they've proven to us the level of betrayal that they're capable of. We are reluctant to place ourselves or our families in that vulnerable position again. But not so with the Lord. When a soul comes to him with a humble, contrite heart, he, quite literally, starts their relationship all over again. God is willing to reside in the temple of that soul's heart, to place himself in the position of that kind of vulnerability, because for him, it is as if the transgressions — the years of betrayal — never happened. God's mercy is so overflowing and all-encompassing, we can scarcely wrap our minds around it.

I trust in the LORD; my soul trusts in his word.

So God's lesson today is one of great mercy; it's not "unfair" at all! And yet ... for the souls we love who have turned away, in order for them to receive God's abundant mercy, there's a giant *if*:

> ... *unless your righteousness surpasses that of the scribes and Pharisees, you will not enter into the Kingdom of heaven.*

Um ... we were hoping Jesus would settle for a barely-hanging-in-there change of heart. Why must our loved one, who is already struggling, "surpass" anyone who is already on board? Because the "surpassing" Jesus asks of them — and us — is not a surpassing of pious practices, but rather, a surpassing of *mercy*:

> ... *go first and be reconciled with your brother, and then come and offer your gift.*

The Pharisees were great at following all the rules, it is true; but there were some that failed to do the one thing necessary:

> ... *to love [God] with all your heart, with all your understanding, with all your strength, and to love your neighbor as yourself* ... (Mk 12:33)

Now it is true, to love God and neighbor is going to entail a whole lot of change of heart, and an overhaul in the way one has been living one's life. To love God with all one's heart is going to necessarily mean an end to all the picking and choosing of only the rules that "feel" good. And to love one's neighbor as oneself is going to mean an end to all the hypocritical finger-pointing and judgment. And all of that is a mighty tall order. We might even be tempted to lose hope ... except for one thing: it is not up to us. It is up to God, and he's already revealed to us his intention:

> ... *he will redeem Israel from all their iniquities* ...

So in the words of Padre Pio, let us "pray, hope, and don't worry." Our prayers and sacrifices will till the soil of our loved ones' hearts to prepare them to receive the graces the Lord has planned for them, in his way and in his time. In the meantime, our job is to "do whatever he tells [us]" (Jn 2:5). We can peacefully trust the Father to bring his own plan to fruition.

But who can discern his errors? Clear thou me from hidden faults. Keep back thy servant also from presumptuous sins; let them not have dominion over me! Then I shall be … innocent of great transgression. (Ps 19:12-13)

SATURDAY OF THE FIRST WEEK OF LENT

(DT 26:16-19; PS 119:1-2, 4-5, 7-8; MT 5:43-48)

You have commanded that your precepts be diligently kept.

It could not have been easy to be an Old Testament Israelite. Thank goodness Jesus came so we do not have to be quite so "diligent" anymore in observing all those many "statutes, commandments and decrees;" one trip to the confessional takes care of all the many times we mess up! How on earth would it have been possible for any one person to remain in the Lord's good graces at all times, let alone an entire race?

Well let's remember that Jesus didn't come to change the law; he came to *fulfill* it. He did not dismiss the old covenant in exchange for a "better" one; he expanded on the one the Father gave us and explained it. This is what Jesus meant in his teaching on "new wineskins."

Jesus, who is mercy itself, died for our sins. Let us thank God for his great mercy. Now if we fail to observe his statutes, ordinances, and decrees, if we willfully turn a deaf ear, preferring that which we want over that which he wants, it takes just *one* turn back, and we can be restored to grace. And, as we learned yesterday, our sins are completely forgotten by God. Easy peasy, right? The thing is, there's a catch. Jesus tells us that if we are truly sorry, he will forgive our sins ... but there's a *new* commandment we must follow, one whose value puts all the others into proper perspective. That new law is this:

> *I give you a new commandment: love one another as I have loved you.* (Jn 13:34)

But wait — what is so new about that? Was not love of neighbor already a commandment followed by the Jews, as evidenced by Jesus's answer to the Pharisees' question on which "commandment in the law" was greatest (Mt 22:36)? Absolutely. But here is where Jesus explains just what that old law now means. To the early Jews, their "neighbor" was literally the people around them; that is, their friends and family. A "neighbor" was a person they already happened to like. So to love one such as this could have been somewhat guided by feelings. Admittedly, that would present a challenge during heated political debates when friends and family gathered around the Passover holiday table, or when a husband and wife were in lousy moods; but as difficult as a commandment such as that would have been, it would not have been impossible. But now Jesus was asking for something different (or at least, clarifying their understanding). Jesus, who came to fulfill the law, does not ask us to do less just because he offers us the Sacrament of Reconciliation. It's the other way around. Because we now have the opportunity to "confidently approach the throne of grace" (Heb 4:16), Jesus requires of us *more*:

> *You have heard that it was said, "You shall love your neighbor and hate your enemy." But I say to you, love your enemies, and pray for those who persecute you.*

If the Father commanded the ancient Jews that which was difficult, but not impossible, Jesus is now asking of them the *impossible*. But why? Why would the Savior set us up for failure by requiring of us that which we cannot do? Because despite their righteousness in fulfilling the law of Moses with "diligence," and despite the new wineskin that Jesus was offering by dying for our sins, some of the faithful still lacked one thing, without which they would never reach eternal Paradise: *humility*. Humility would only come to them by way of spiritual poverty, and that kind of poverty would only come by way of their recognizing their utter dependence upon God. They needed to acknowledge that without his grace, they were *nothing*. They needed to acknowledge that they would *never* be able to fulfill God's laws, unless it was his spirit within them moving their own. This was the new wineskin. Jesus clarified what the definition of "perfection" would be from thenceforth.

> *... be perfect, just as your heavenly Father is perfect.*

To be "perfect," then, would mean nothing more on our part, then that we acknowledge our sinfulness, helplessness, and our dependance upon God, and that we persevere in striving to follow the commandments more faithfully.

> *It is not that I have already taken hold of it or have already attained perfect maturity, but I continue my pursuit in hope that I may possess it ... forgetting what lies behind but straining forward to what lies ahead, I continue my pursuit toward the goal ...* (Phil 3:12,16)

If we "recognize, trust, and try" (Fr. Michael Gaitley, *33 Days to Merciful Love*), Jesus will forgive us our transgressions and perfect us in his grace. He makes us shiny and new! And yet ... these steps sound rather self-oriented. How does focusing on personal holiness translate into loving our enemy and praying for those who persecute us?

> *Remain in my love. If you keep my commandments, you will remain in my love ...* (Jn 15:9-10)

There is something about humbly acknowledging our failings and loving and trusting Jesus by giving him praise and thanks in all things, which results in the grace-filled consequence of loving our enemies. Why? Because as we see our own sinfulness for what it is, we begin to look less at the sinful behavior of others and more at their wound. Like Jesus, we begin to have compassion on them in their offense. We begin to see them no longer as our "enemy," but as our brother, because, in our honest assessment of ourselves, we see that our own personal wounds have caused us to behave, at times, just like them. And as that understanding of the bigger picture begins to take root, forgiveness starts to seep into our hearts, not just as a begrudging act of the will, but in all sincerity, because it transpires within us by way of God's *grace.* If we remain childlike and humble, in his love, it is *Jesus* who will keep us in his commandments, loving him with all our heart, mind and soul, and loving our neighbor as he loves us.

> *... provided you keep all his commandments ... you will be a people sacred to the* LORD, *your God, as he promised.*

SECOND SUNDAY OF LENT

GN 12:1-4; PS 33:4-5, 18-20, 22; 2 TM 1:8B-10; MT 17:1-9 (YEAR A)
GN 22: 1-2, 9-13, 15-18; PS 116: 10, 15-19; ROM 8: 31-34; MK 9: 2-10 (YEAR B)
GN 15:5-12, 17-18; PS 27: 1, 7-9, 13-14; PHIL 3:17-4:1; LK 9: 28-36 (YEAR C)

Isaac continued, "Here are the fire and the wood, but where is the sheep for the holocaust?" "Son," Abraham answered, "God himself will provide the sheep for the holocaust." (Gn 22:7-8)

What a strange scene here. Yes, this is an incredible testimony to the steadfast faith that Abraham has for the Father in heaven that he should be willing to sacrifice his own son in obedience to God's will, but … did he just *lie* to Isaac? We can reason that Abraham perhaps figuratively refers to Isaac as the "sheep," or that his rather cryptic response to Isaac's question is a merciful attempt to prevent his son from undue anxiety over the inevitable; still, it's strange. Couldn't Abraham have chosen to answer his son's question gently, but also plainly? And yet, it gets stranger:

Abraham built an altar there and arranged the wood on it. Next he tied up his son Isaac, and put him on top of the wood on the altar. Then he reached out and took the knife to slaughter his son.

La la la la la … "next he tied up his son." This elderly senior citizen is tying up his full grown son? How on earth does he manage that? One would think Isaac could have taken his father down with one hand tied behind his back. No, the only way Abraham could have accomplished such a monumental task is if

Isaac offered himself *willingly*. Which would suggest that Abraham is not the only one in this story with the supernatural grace of obedience and trust. Isaac too displays the same kind of steadfast faith that he learned from his father. It is entirely possible that Isaac understood *exactly* what Abraham meant in response to his question about the missing sacrificial sheep. And he would have understood that this perplexing and agonizing command was coming not from Abraham, but rather, from God himself.

I believed, even when I said, "I am greatly afflicted."

If we want to know the secret to receiving God's mercy and peace *always*, no matter what the circumstance, then we have but one course of action we must undertake at every moment of every day: strive to see the hand of God in our circumstance. The only time we will ever place ourselves in a position to veer off course is if we choose to believe that what we are experiencing is somehow outside of God's will. That mentality will always lead us to rebel, to take matters into our own hands, which will necessarily make a mess of things. That is not to say that God calls us to inaction, to do "nothing" until he finally decides to fix things. Rather, seeing his hand in our circumstances is a very much *active* trust: a certainty that if we've placed our lives in his hands, if we've asked him from the bottom of our hearts to take care of it, then no matter how things turn out, we can surely trust that it *is* God's will. We don't have to try a different novena, find a different faith healer, or go to a particular place of pilgrimage (unless God calls us to, of course). Trust begets us the grace to know with certainty that however things turn out, it is the best possible way, whether we can understand our circumstances right now or not.

For my thoughts are not your thoughts, nor are your ways my ways, says the LORD. (Is 55:8)

God teaches the simple this wisdom of mercy and trust *so that* this message gets passed on to others. If we want to transform our world, then this is our only mission. It's urgent ... and it's beautiful. If we can bring peace to our tiny corner of this wounded world by pointing out God's providential action in the lives of others, then that is all we need do to spread a balm of healing that will extend to all the earth.

O Lord I am your servant … the son of your handmaid …

MONDAY OF THE SECOND WEEK OF LENT

(DN 9:4-10; PS 79:8, 9, 11, 13; LK 6:36-38)

For the measure with which you measure will in return be measured out to you.

St. Colette is somewhat of a lesser-known saint in the Church. Perhaps she is best remembered for her reformation of the Poor Clare Nuns in the 15th century. St. Colette succeeded not only in reforming the existing convents, but also in founding seventeen new ones — an undertaking that was impressive enough. But what is really fascinating about her tale is that her work was sanctioned not by the holy vicar of Christ, but by the then anti-pope, Benedict XIII of Avignon. Of course, dozens of questions arise for us, not the least of which is: how could God allow his children the divisive and agonizing confusion and controversy of having to sort between an anti-pope and the true pope of his sacred Church? What's more, how could a saint, as holy and pure as St. Colette, seek guidance and instruction from one who was not in legitimate authority to her? Suffice it to say, it is a mystery. But the first lesson we learn from Collette's life is that God's grace can work miracles despite any corruption or dysfunction that enters in. Corruption and dysfunction certainly present obstacles to us in our physical lives, but they are not obstacles to God. The only thing that can get in the way of God's grace in our lives is our lack of faith. Conversely, what welcomes the grace of God into our lives is our obedient trust. So if things seem to be going from bad to worse, let us learn from St. Colette: this is the time to increase our trust. Let us praise and thank God with even greater determination.

> *... a good measure [of gifts], packed together, shaken down, and overflowing, will be poured into your lap ...*

The reward to St. Colette for giving God all the trust in her heart was an abundance of grace. But the grace she received was not meant to be kept just for herself; it was meant to be "measured" out through her heart upon others! What's more, for Collette, that giving of herself would have been no burden at all; it would have been both her mission and her greatest love, because it was a mission entrusted to her by Jesus. As such, the consequence of giving herself away would have been profound peace and joy, though these would not have been her motivation for accomplishing what the Lord set her out to do. Colette would have done it anyway, even if she had experienced dryness and abandonment until the day she drew her dying breath. Such would have been her faith. Such would have been her love.

But what about Benedict XIII of Avignon? God clearly used him in his plan for St. Colette's mission. What, then, was measured out upon this anti-pope, in return for that which he measured out upon others?

> *We have not obeyed your servants the prophets ... you have scattered them because of their treachery toward you ...*

There was a sincere belief on the part of this anti-pope that he was the true vicar of Christ. The cardinals elected him after all, did they not? The thing is, they elected him *after* they had already legitimately elected Pope Urban VI, who, to their dismay, proved to be hostile toward them. Further research would be required to understand what exactly this hostility towards them entailed, but suffice it to say, some of the cardinals decided they had made a mistake. These few cardinals took it upon themselves to reconvene, declare the earlier election invalid (perhaps because of the intense pressure the people of Rome had placed on the cardinals to elect an Italian pope so that the papacy would not end up back in Avignon), and so this subset of cardinals held a re-election. Thus, the chair of the anti-pope was borne. And we think there's drama in our Church today!

The result of all this convolution was the "Western Schism," a sad time in our Church's history, and one that persisted for decades. Did Benedict XIII of Avignon ever have a change of heart? Sadly, it appears not. Benedict refused to abdicate his papal seat in Avignon. It would seem that Benedict was never able to see the harm and division his pride had caused. Benedict didn't steal, he didn't lie, he didn't cheat, and he didn't kill. In the eyes of the world, for all intents and purposes, he was a "good" man. But because of his blind pride, he is remembered by the Church for his stubbornness. Benedict XIII of Avignon has gone down in history as the man who slashed our Church in two. Unlike Colette, who was measured out a heart full of love and peace and joy in return for her generous measure given away, Benedict was measured out a heart of envy, resentment, anger, jealousy, greed, dissatisfaction, agitation, distress, discord. He would have lived a hell on earth, even before his eternal fate was judged.

Justice, O Lord, is on your side …

Which leaves us with just one question. How could it have come to this for this man, and for the people who supported him, who likely had a genuine, though misguided, desire to protect the "true" faith? The reason this question is so important to ask is not simply out of curiosity or for the sake of interest in that historical period of the Church. The reason this question is important to ask is because of the period of the Church in which we are living *now*. The reality is, things are not so different in our Church today. There is no shortage of "cardinals against cardinals" and "bishops against bishops" (Our Lady of Akita), some of whom even oppose the very Pope himself. So what can we learn from our shameful past to ensure that history doesn't repeat itself?

> "Oh, how sweet and pleasant to that soul and to Me is holy prayer, made in the house of knowledge of self and of Me, opening the eye of the intellect to the light of faith ..." —St. Catherine of Siena

The "eye of our intellect" will only open to the truth and "light of our faith" if we offer a very specific kind of prayer to God. After all, we can assume Benedict of Avignon was praying. We can assume the cardinals who elected him were praying. We can assume the people who supported him were praying. We can assume, in all the divisions we have experienced in our Church today, that most of us faithful Christians are praying. So why are we not all on the same page? Because, according to the words of Jesus to St. Catherine of Siena, the only kind of prayer that will "open the eye of our intellect" to the "light of our faith" is the one which is made "in the house of knowledge of self and of [him]." In other words, we must strive to recognize our own weakness before we can understand the weakness of others. We must point the finger inward first if we want to understand the behavior of others. In a word, humility is the only kind of prayer our Lord responds to. Without humility, we will not hear his voice, because our souls will simply not be listening.

There is a part two to our humble prayer: the fruit of such prayer is a greater knowledge of Christ. Why? Because the more we grow in the awareness of our own sinfulness, the more we understand our need for his mercy. And as we receive that mercy, our heart begins to burn with the desire to share that same mercy with others. That measure really is packed down and overflowing — such that we can no longer contain it within ourselves! We start to look less at the hurtful behavior of those who harm us, and more at their wound. And it is our love and mercy for souls that begins to win over their hearts, more than anything else we could possibly do. Like St. Colette, let us strive always to give what we have, that "the measure with which [we] measure [may] in return be measured out to [us]."

TUESDAY OF THE SECOND WEEK OF LENT

(ROM 8:31B-39; PS 124:2-8; MT 10:34-39)

If God is for us, who can be against us?

Perpetua and Felicity are two saints whom the Church recognizes for their heroic virtue; their lives are certainly examples of courage and faith for the rest of us to admire, no doubt. But here's the thing. You know when you read about those ancient saints who are thrown into a wild animal's den for being Christians, but then are miraculously spared? That did not happen to Perpetua and Felicity. Oh, they were thrown into the animal's den all right. And then *mauled* to death. Where was God's supernatural bubble of protection then? If God was "for" those two, he sure did not do a great job protecting them from the ones who were "against" them!

Whoever finds his life will lose it, and whoever loses his life for my sake will find it.

Of course, our faith tells us that Perpetua and Felicity were rewarded abundantly in the hereafter, making their suffering on earth as nothing compared to the glory they now experience in eternity. The blip that was their life on earth has no bearing upon their rejoicing *now*. When we suffer, the memory of that suffering can cause us pain, even when we are no longer undergoing the trial. But for Perpetua and Felicity, the memory of their suffering carries with it only joy, as they are keenly and supernaturally aware of the fact that every ounce of sacrifice offered to Christ led them to the glory they experience now and forevermore. They would not go back and change a thing, even if they could.

Whoever does not take up his cross and follow after me is not worthy of me.

Now that is all well and good for the angels and saints in heaven who have that clarity of vision ... but how does God expect the rest of us old blokes to go skipping down the lane on the path that leads to martyrdom, smiling and whistling show tunes along the way? After all, God *might* hold back the savage mouths of the lions, like he did for Daniel. On the other hand ... He might *not*, as we see was the case for today's two saints. I don't know that I could honestly say if I were standing in Perpetua's and Felicity's shoes, I wouldn't try to run away and escape such fate. Or worse, would I cave in fear and deny my faith altogether to avoid the horrific torture and death that awaited me? Such a response would be both human and understandable. After all, God is the one who created us with the innate instinct to live! And yet ... at the same, he calls us to be willing to sacrifice our lives for his sake. How can this be possible? There is only one way. It is the way that Perpetua and Felicity found, and it's the way we're called to find in our own lives as well:

"Then I realized that I would not fight against wild animals, but against the devil …" – St. Perpetua

The vision these two saints beheld from heaven — the hand of God in all things, that all things work for good, that every choice we make in life matters, good or bad, and that our actions affect the entire body of Christ, for better or for worse — was a vision they had already put into practice during their lives on earth. They would have spent their lives striving for it, day in and day out, so that by the time they reached the point where the rubber meets the road, they were *prepared.* No, they did not face that animal's den joyfully by their own human strength. Nobody could. But after persevering in practicing the virtue of trust, their souls were in a disposition to receive the grace of God precisely at the moment when they needed it most. These ladies were *sincerely* joyful. They were not crazy or pretending; nor was this an exaggerated account recorded as the legend was passed, word of mouth, down the generations. When Perpetua and Felicity walked calmly into that arena, they could truly *see.*

> *What will separate us from the love of Christ? Will anguish, or distress, or persecution, or famine, or nakedness, or peril, or the sword? ... No, in all these things we conquer overwhelmingly through him who loved us.*

Friends, we can spend an awful lot of time on "what if." But there is a very specific reason that "what if" is a waste of time, and it's not only because the things we worry about may never come to pass. The reality is ... they very well might. But the reason that worrying about our inability to handle a hypothetical situation is a waste of time is that God doesn't give us graces for things we don't need in the present moment. However, he *showers* us with the graces we do need, *if* we prepare ahead of time, by placing ourselves in a disposition to receive those graces. That is, by praising him and thanking him in all things, and striving to see his hand in all our circumstances.

One winter, a 19-year-old young woman in our community died in a car accident. I had met her mother years before, and that connection, albeit distant, brought the tragedy a little too close to home for me. The thought that anything could happen to any of my kids at any time is scarcely more than I can bear. This mother was a faithful woman! How could God have allowed this to happen to her? What is the point of us praying for him to protect our children if he could allow such a tragedy? But then … a good friend who attended the young woman's funeral had this to say about it:

"It was BEAUTIFUL. Perfect."

Only God could make something so tragic both "beautiful" and "perfect." Only one who has received his abundant, overflowing, unimaginable grace will have eyes to see that beauty and that perfection. And once that happens, a soul really and truly accepts — in a sense, equally — both the joys as well as the sorrows in life, as did Saints Perpetua and Felicity. Such souls see only the eternity that is to come and have already begun to live that eternity here on earth.

> "[Love] alone can make our burdens light, and alone it bears in equal balance what is pleasing and displeasing. It carries a burden and does not feel it; it makes all that is bitter taste sweet. Nothing is sweeter than love… [The souls of] such lovers are free." —Thomas à Kempis

WEDNESDAY OF THE SECOND WEEK OF LENT

(JER 18:18-20; PS 31:5-6, 14-16; MT 20:17-28)

Must good be repaid with evil ...?

In Jeremiah's case, the answer to his own question seems to be "yes." Of all the prophets of the Bible, Jeremiah's story has to be the most ... well, disheartening. This is a man who prophesied through no less than four kings, over the course of *forty* years, warning the people of Israel to change their ways ... to *no* avail. The people did not listen, but what they *could* hear was a lot of irritating and bothersome squawking on the part of a man who, it seemed to them, was trying to ruin all their fun and take away the pleasures they enjoyed. But after forty years of this, the people were past being irritated. To them, his prophecies were both discouraging and obnoxious. They decided it was time for Jeremiah to *go.*

The people of Judah and the citizens of Jerusalem said, "Come, let us contrive a plot against Jeremiah."

So the plan was to throw Jeremiah into a cistern of mud and starve him to death. He did eventually get rescued ... but let's stop right here for a minute. Can we even imagine what must have been going through Jeremiah's heart in that moment — alone, stuck in filth and stench, with no apparent way out? Did God give him the supernatural grace to sing hymns of joy, the way Maximilian Kolbe did in the concentration camp at Auschwitz? Hardly. Jeremiah was in a pit, both physically and mentally:

> *Woe to me, my mother, that you have borne me, a man of strife and conflict in all the land. I have neither lent nor borrowed, yet everyone curses me …* (Jer 15:10)

After his rescue from the cistern, Jeremiah was thrown into prison, and once released from prison, he was then exiled to Egypt where he lived the rest of his days, against his will. The End. Well, that's a crummy story! How are we supposed to gain any encouragement from *that*? After all, Jeremiah spent his *whole* life warning the people to change their ways ... the result of which ended in *failure* until the day he took his dying breath. Ok yes, he is in heaven now, all is well for Jeremiah at this point. But, other than eternity, what could possibly have been gained from all the suffering he endured in life, if no one else was changed by it?

Jeremiah is the one prophet who shows us that to do God's will "because God says so" is the only reason we need. Certainly, the omniscient God would have known that Jeremiah's efforts would have resulted in naught for the people who he relentlessly warned. So why did the Lord put him through all that? Was this really all one giant test, with no relief or reward at all for as long as Jeremiah walked the earth? Perhaps. But God's intentions are never worthless or fruitless, and so we must ask ourselves the question: what fruit came from the prophecies of Jeremiah? Perhaps we can understand the answer to that question if we seek to first understand for *whom* his prophecies were intended. It is true, Jeremiah spoke his words *to* the people of ancient Israel, and eventually to the Jews in Egypt once he was exiled there. But his words were meant *for* the people who would listen ... centuries later. His words were meant for *us*. When Jeremiah warned the people that if they did not turn their hearts back to the Lord, Jerusalem would fall, it seemed like a nonsensical figment of his imagination (much as if someone had warned us in 2019 that the entire *world* would be shut down the following year). So, nobody believed Jeremiah. But unlike the ancient Israelites, we have the benefit of history which tells us that what Jeremiah warned about — the unthinkable — did take place. What's more, for those of us now living in a post-pandemic era, we've seen for ourselves that the "unthinkable" can take place at any time! What is God saying to us now? The same message he was conveying through his prophet Jeremiah:

> *Even now, says the LORD, return to me with your whole heart.* (Jl 2:12)

Now because of the era in which he lived, unlike Maximilian Kolbe, Jeremiah did not have hope in a resurrected Christ. He really and truly saw abysmal failure alone:

> *You have deceived me, O LORD, and I was deceived. You have overcome me and prevailed. I am a laughingstock all day long; everyone mocks me* … (Jer 20:7)

So what kept him going amidst all that dejection and despondency? After all, he certainly wasn't hanging onto the pillar of hope and optimism that people cling to for encouragement to persevere. Well, there was one rather unusual gift given to him by the Lord, one that essentially "forced" Jeremiah not to give up and quit:

> *... whenever I speak, I cry out, I proclaim violence and destruction. For the word of the LORD has become to me a reproach and derision all day long. If I say, "I will not mention him or speak any more in his name," his message becomes a fire burning in my heart, shut up in my bones, and I become weary of holding it in, and I cannot prevail* … (Jer 20:8-9)

There was not one ounce of Jeremiah that desired to keep prophesying against this hostile crowd. He, more than anyone, just wanted to retire and be left alone. But God made it so that to not speak would feel a whole lot worse than it did *to* speak. Now why would God do that? Because Jeremiah's mission was such that there was simply not going to be anything about it that would *feel* good. A reward was simply not to be had by him for as long as he walked the earth. The only incentive for him to persevere would have been, then, that if he were to give up, the agony would be far more than he could bear. How's that for a "blessing" from a loving Father!

Well, thankfully, we are not all called to walk in Jeremiah's shoes, but we are all called to learn from him. The first lesson we learn, as we have already said, is that if we did not pay attention to his prophecy before, let's make sure we heed it now. We must return to the Lord with all our *hearts*. That is, by continually taking that humble look inward, acknowledging our sinfulness, and trusting in his providence. We cannot just do him lip service by checking off boxes from the piety list. Of course, for those of us sincerely striving for holiness, by now we already are trying to acknowledge and trust, though it is true that we are weak, and we are sinful.

But there is a second lesson we learn from Jeremiah, and it has less to do with our role as "listeners" and more to do with our role as "prophets." Yes, *prophets*! We, too, as followers of Christ, must proclaim his message in season and out of season, when it is convenient and inconvenient, when it is popular and unpopular. We must proclaim his message, even when no one is heeding it. And even when we are mocked, scorned, and rejected for it.

My chalice you will indeed drink…

Wow, sounds pretty heavy. Divisive even! The thing is, if we are screaming, berating, judging, condemning, or losing our temper ... none of this is what it means to be a prophet of the Lord. To speak for Christ means we speak *in* Christ. That is, it is Christ who does the speaking through us. When we "decrease" so that Jesus may "increase" (Jn 3:30), when it is he who "lives" and "moves" and is our "being" (Acts 17:28), then there is never reason for us to lose our patience, our temper, our peace, or our trust. We do "whatever he tells us" (Jn 2:5) … nothing less, but also nothing more. It is true, we might not have the benefit of seeing instant results. We might not have the benefit of seeing *any* results. But results are not what Jesus always intends for us to see. We must leave outcomes to him, because sometimes the purpose of our actions will not be revealed until later — sometimes even *centuries* later, as in the case of Jeremiah. Sometimes the people we think our words and actions are intended for are not necessarily the ones for whom the Lord intends them. So, while God may not always reveal his results to us, he *will* always reveal to us his hand in our circumstances, if we but ask him to. It is this that will give us the encouragement we need to keep going. To do otherwise, after all, would feel so much worse.

THURSDAY OF THE SECOND WEEK OF LENT

(JER 17:5-10; PS 1:1-4, 6; LK 16:19-3)

Abraham replied, "My child, remember that you received what was good during your lifetime while Lazarus likewise received what was bad; but now he is comforted here, whereas you are tormented."

As a child growing up in the 70's, to me, it always seemed that World War II was ages ago, a distant memory, something that haunted generations of the past, but was not particularly pertinent to our modern generation, enlightened a people as we are. But now that I am older ... goodness, World War II was not nearly as long ago as my little childhood brain was imagining. At the time of my birth, there was a large contingent of people who lived through the atrocities of World War II. This was no "distant memory" for them, nor was it something that happened to "other people." Corrie Ten Boom once wrote about the untold suffering of war, "We need to think about that when we sit down in our nice houses with our nice clothes to eat our steak dinners." It is really difficult, if not impossible, to wrap one's mind around the unimaginable devastation of war and still enjoy a vacation at the beach or a frivolous shopping trip without a care in the world. So most of the time, we don't think about it.

Lazarus, covered with sores ... would gladly have eaten his fill of the scraps that fell from the rich man's table.

In Jesus's parable, Lazarus knew what it was to endure horror. He was starving, covered with sores, and living in abject poverty. But Jesus tells us that Lazarus made it to the eternal reward our lives on earth are intended for. Now the rich man, who was comforted on earth with the juicy steaks, the vacations to the beach, and the frivolous shopping trips, did not end up in Paradise. Even his very name was forgotten, left unwritten in the "book of life" (Rev 21:27). So what does this tell us? That only those whose lives on earth stink get to go to heaven, whereas those who actually enjoy their earthly lives go to hell? That is a frightening thought for those of us who happen to like both steak and the beach; what's more, it sounds a little like Jesus is relating this story just to make the misfortunate feel better.

Blessed is the man who trusts in the LORD, whose hope is the LORD.

The reality is, Jesus used Lazarus as an extreme example of one who suffered without reprieve, not to show us that we must never enjoy a day in our lives if we want to make it to heaven, but rather, to show us the one thing that *is* required to get to heaven, regardless of our circumstances: *humility.* Now Lazarus was not automatically humble simply because he was poor and covered with sores. After all, disadvantaged people are not immune to pride. Sometimes their pride prevents them from admitting, "This is more than I can handle; I can't do this alone." They put on a mask of pretense, but everyone knows they are struggling because their disposition belies their words: people such as these are generally angry and bitter, and in the end, anger and bitterness is something a person simply cannot hide. Lazarus, on the other hand, had no such disposition. It is true, Scripture does not reveal to us whether he spent his days complaining, nor does it reveal just how grumpy he was or was not. But there is one important detail we are told about Lazarus, and it speaks volumes:

... lying at his door was ... Lazarus ... Dogs even used to come and lick his sores.

Lazarus, who "*was* lying" down, and for whom dogs "*used* to come," had been waiting at the rich man's door day after day. This was not a one-time event, otherwise we would have heard that he "lay" at the door (past tense), and not that he "was lying" (past progressive); we would have heard that dogs "came," and not that they "used to come." In other words, his waiting by the door was an ongoing event. Why is this important to know? Because it tells us that Lazarus did not give up. He did not lose hope. He persevered in trusting that God would hear his prayer, that perhaps today would be the day, against all odds. He would have sensed that God wanted him exactly where he was, even though he could not understand why, and even though the results of his prayers were different from what he had hoped. Lazarus was a man of faith, a man of trust, and a man of great humility.

But there is one other detail Scripture tells us about Lazarus that seals the deal for him when it comes to his final judgement:

Lazarus ... would GLADLY have eaten his fill of the scraps that fell ...

Lazarus was both joyful as well as grateful. This was a servant who *pleased* the Father, because his joy did not come from his circumstances, but from God alone. Lazarus learned the secret of seeking "not the consolation of God, but the God of consolations" (St. Bernard). Like Jesus, Lazarus's "food" truly was to do the will of the Father (Jn 4:34). It was his *response* to his illness and poverty, then, and not the illness and poverty itself, that gained him his eternal reward.

I, the LORD, alone probe the mind and test the heart ... To reward everyone according to his ways, according to the merit of his deeds.

But what about the rich man? After all, Scripture doesn't tell us he was a "bad" man; in fact, this man sincerely wished to be in heaven now that his eyes were opened. Furthermore, there was at least enough charity in his heart, such that he desired his brothers to avoid his same fate. That certainly does not sound selfish! What was so bad about this man's wealth and entertainment that landed him a spot in the place of eternal torment? Of course, like Lazarus, it was not his circumstances that "caused" his eternal damnation; it was his *response* to his circumstances. In all probability, this rich man didn't make the conscious decision not to feed a starving man. The reality is, he likely didn't even *notice* him. How is that possible? Because when our lives are filled with steak and the beach and shopping, we have a tendency to be *distracted.* We do not pray quite as ardently as we do when we're suffering. We are not quite as aware of our utter need for God in the times in which we have everything we could possibly want. Friends, we spend so much of our lives wishing we did not have such and such problem to worry about, yearning for the day we no longer have to face the difficulties with which we currently struggle, looking forward to weekends, vacations, retirement ... and that's all understandable. It's just that, if we're looking for God, it's going to be a whole lot harder to find him in an existence that is problem-free. This is why it is "easier for a camel to pass through the eye of a needle than for one who is rich to enter the kingdom of God" (Mt 19:24). We simply are not wired to have all our needs met and still need God too. That is the whole reason the Church in her wisdom urges us to give things up for Lent. Jesus does indeed want our joy to be "complete," but paradoxically, that kind of joy will only come about if we experience what it means to be deprived.

In those times when our merciful Lord sends a trial (or two) our way, let us thank him for it in all sincerity, and not just as a begrudging act of the will. Our suffering and our trials are a sure sign to us that Jesus is calling us close.

> *You shall love the Lord, your God, with all your heart, with all your soul, and with all your mind. This is the greatest and the first commandment. The second is like it: You shall love your neighbor as yourself. The whole law and the prophets depend on these two commandments…* (Mt 22:37-40)

FRIDAY OF THE SECOND WEEK OF LENT

(GN 37:3-4, 12-13A, 17B-28A; PS 105:16-21; MT 21:33-43, 45-46)

When his brothers saw that their father loved him best of all his sons, they hated him so much that they would not even greet him.

The account of Joseph's life has more twists and turns than just about any other story in the Bible. And there are a lot of twisted tales in Scripture! The first thing we read about Joseph is that he was his father's "favorite." This favoritism drew the ire of his older brothers. Now we can certainly understand the jealousy that might have been provoked in them, especially if their father was constantly giving Joseph special gifts, letting him get away with not doing certain chores while the other boys all had to do their share, always talking about how smart and handsome and funny and charming he was, while totally ignoring all the other siblings in their efforts to please and impress him. Of course, Scripture does not tell us this was the behavior of their father Jacob, but whatever his behavior was, it was enough to make all the brothers feel that they did not matter to him as much as Joseph did. So we really do understand their temptation to jealousy. And yet, "jealousy" is not the word Scripture uses to describe them. When the Pharisees tested and plotted against Jesus, we are told their behavior was a result of their jealousy. But today we are told Joseph's brothers plotted against him because "they hated him so much." Is there really a difference? Well, yes. In the case of the Pharisees, their jealousy came from the things Jesus was saying and doing, threatening to take away their power and position. In today's very Gospel, for example, Jesus tells the Pharisees, "The Kingdom of God will be taken away from you and given to a people that will produce its fruit." And the Pharisees "knew that he was speaking about them." Talk about giving rise to another's ire! The plotting started as a direct result of a perceived attack. But in the case of Joseph's brothers, there was no such "attack." It is true, Joseph related to them a couple of obnoxious dreams about them bowing down to him, but those dreams only made them hate him "all the *more*." In other words, they hated him before a word about his dreams was ever even spoken to them. What's more, their hatred, besides being uncharitable, was also unwarranted. Scripture tells us that Jacob loved Joseph best of all "*for* he was the child of his old age." "For," meaning, "because." In other words, Jacob "favored" Joseph *because* Jacob was an old man, and Joseph was the baby; he had legitimate reason to feel the way he did! Now I have had ten children myself, so I know a thing or two about a parent trying to give of herself equally to each one. It does not happen. At least not all at the same time. During this season, one needs you more, during that season, another. Some children get your attention simply because they are more demanding; others tend to get less because they like to fly under the radar. But do you know who always gets plenty of attention? The *baby*. When I had baby number ten, like Jacob, I was *old*. My doctor said that out of all the patients he had ever personally attended to, I was the patient most advanced in age to conceive naturally! I remember thinking what a miraculous gift from God that was. Of course, all babies are miracles, but I knew in my heart this one was *special*, because he could easily not have been here. It was an act of God that he was.

When Joseph was born, Jacob was old too. He had been given the gift of new life long past the time he'd thought possible. For him, it was a miracle. So he's overwhelmed with gratitude. What's more, this baby is the firstborn son of his second wife Rachel, the woman whom he loves like none other — including the mother of his older children, Leah. And herein lies the crux of the seed of hatred that was brewing in the hearts of his sons. If Joseph had been the "baby" of their own mother, he could have been a brat, prone to temper tantrums and demanding constant attention ... and do you know what? They would have loved him just as much as their father did. That he was the "favorite" would not have bothered them one bit; they would have laughed about it, completely understood it, and even felt the same way themselves. As grown adult men, nothing would have changed how they felt about their little brother, not even his pompous, annoying dreams. At worst, they would have shrugged at those dreams and moved on; at best, they may have even listened. Joseph was, after all, the *baby* (at least until Benjamin came along). But instead, Jacob's favoritism for Joseph was, for the brothers, an affront to their mother Leah. It was this they would not have been able to get past. All those years that Jacob had been married to Leah would have seemed to them as if forgotten by their father the moment Joseph was born. Being fertile was the one thing Leah had over Rachel, the only leverage she'd had over her sister since she could never compete with Jacob's love for her; and now, with the birth of Joseph, that sole leverage was gone.

It is quite likely that the hatred these brothers felt for Joseph was planted in their hearts long before he was even born. Perhaps the hatred they imposed on him was in actuality a transference of the resentment Leah felt for her sister Rachel, who was favored by her own husband. There was nothing Leah could ever say or do to win over the affection of his heart — not even the bearing of his children. Leah's whole life would have been spent serving this man as a faithful wife, though she would have known her own father had tricked Jacob into marrying her and would have been well aware that Jacob did not love her from the start of their marriage. But after all the children she bore him, she would have grown to love Jacob, and would have hoped, in the end, that he might love her too.

Of course, Scripture does not offer us this explanation. We just don't know for sure what precipitated all that hatred in the hearts of siblings who should have looked at their baby brother as the apple of their eyes. But we can still learn something from the brothers' relationship with Joseph in today's reading. Perhaps we ourselves can't think of anyone for whom we harbor such outright hatred ... but all of us sure can understand the feeling of resentment. Of course, there are things that explain our resentment: past wounds, arrogance on the other's part, unfair treatment, or just plain irritating behavior ... but *still.* What makes it so hard for us to let go? Especially when we are trying so hard to follow in the footsteps of a forgiving, merciful Christ? Perhaps it is this we need to explore more deeply, because while the behavior of others can certainly explain our own response to them, it doesn't excuse it, nor does it *cause* it. What seeds have been planted in our own hearts that have tainted our vision so that the face of Christ is obscured for us in the face of the one we struggle to love? What lies have we come to believe that have squelched and covered the truth that has been written deep within our hearts? Let's uncover those truths today. Let's begin to understand where our feelings of "hatred" come from so that, unlike the brothers who did nothing to stop it, we can be set free from it before it's too late. We just might find that the ones who we are rejecting are the very ones God has chosen to lead us to salvation. Let us learn to embrace the fact that they are in our lives with love, and even with joy. Like Joseph was for his brothers, they may just be our cornerstone.

> "If I were to meet the slave traders who kidnapped me and even those who tortured me, I would kneel and kiss their hands, for if that did not happen, I would not be a Christian and religious today." – St. Josephine Bakhita

SATURDAY OF THE SECOND WEEK OF LENT

(MI 7:14-15, 18-20; PS 103:1-4, 9-12; LK 15:1-3, 11-32)

... the Pharisees and scribes began to complain, saying, "This man welcomes sinners and eats with them." So to them Jesus addressed this parable.

In today's Gospel, "tax collectors and sinners" are all drawing close to Jesus, eager to listen to him preach and teach. Evidently, whatever teachings they had previously received from the other Rabbis at the synagogue didn't touch their hearts and move them to conversion, the way Jesus's words did. It would seem that the only thing they had previously received from those in religious authority to them was a feeling of unmistakable condemnation and resolute unwelcome. They were even referred to by the Pharisees simply as "sinner." Now if I were the neighborhood gossip, I might tell you the guy who lives at the house across the street cheats on his taxes, and the one who lives at the house next door is having an affair ... but wouldn't it seem odd if I just labeled them both as *sinner*? One wonders what that word even meant to a first century Jew. Was a sinner someone who committed a sin so vile to his community that to speak its name would be an abomination itself? Not likely. After all, the crowd gathered there were perfectly willing to pick up their stones and call out the sins of a woman caught in adultery, naming it for what it was. What's more, the Torah is riddled with such sinners, many in the line of King David himself. So who were the Pharisees referring to when labeling someone a sinner? It seems that "sinner" referred to anyone for whom all 613 laws were too heavy to carry. For one such as this, for whom forgiveness and acceptance from the Pharisees was impossible because following the law down to the letter was impossible, perhaps their transgressions gradually shifted from minor infractions to much more destructive ones, as they lost hope of being welcomed back to the Jewish community they had loved and cherished. Perhaps they gained at least some form of acceptance in being part of a community that was labeled in the same category as theirs. So by the time Jesus came on the scene, these "sinners," perhaps for the first time in their lives, were being taught by a Rabbi who offered them *hope.* Jesus was offering them a way back *home.*

Now enter the Pharisees, who witness such a disgrace. A disgrace because, for them, these sinners and tax collectors had their chance, they blew it, and now the punishment they deserve is banishment from the Jewish community. Those sinners knew the rules; everybody else had to work with diligence to follow them. Why shouldn't the sinners? What gave them the right to special privileges? And it is here that Jesus turns away from the sinners and tax collectors and turns instead to the Pharisees, addressing the parable of the prodigal son to *them.* The Pharisees are acting jealous and resentful … and what does Jesus have to say to them?

> *My son, you are here with me always; everything I have is yours. But now we must celebrate and rejoice, because your brother was dead and has come to life again; he was lost and has been found.*

Jesus does not end his parable by telling us whether the father and his sons all lived happily ever after, or whether that older son continued to hold onto a resentful grudge. Why does Jesus not let us know the older son's reaction? Perhaps because that son's reaction is not what we need to know to decide what *our* reaction will be. "Everything I have is yours" should be all the words we need to hear to absolutely melt our hearts. These are the tender words of understanding and compassion from a Father who loves all his children equally. This is a statement that reveals that the Father's love for us is not dependent upon what we do or fail to do, and that *nothing* can diminish his love for us. Such a truth should *change* us! It should set us *free*! And it should have melted the hearts of the Pharisees listening to Jesus that day. He was not reprimanding them; he was telling them how much he loved them!

My son ... everything I have is yours.

Jesus does not reveal the older son's response because he was offering the Pharisees now a choice: *What will you decide? Will you welcome your "little brothers" back home, even though they've made mistakes — mistakes that cost both you, and more importantly, your beloved Father dearly? Will you recognize the joy that has now filled your Father's heart, far surpassing the suffering he endured at your brothers' transgressions? Will you allow the humiliation your brothers have undergone to be discipline enough, or will you continue to punish them by your rejection? Will you let My words seep in and melt your hearts, or will your hardness of heart prevent you from letting them in, ever again?*

These are questions we could ask ourselves today, each in our own personal lives. Because the reality is, that kind of mercy does not come naturally to us. As a matter of fact, it is *impossible* ... without God's grace.

Who is there like you, the God who removes guilt and pardons sin ... Who does not persist in anger forever, but delights rather in clemency, and will again have compassion on us, treading underfoot our guilt?

Only God "delights in clemency" and "treads our guilt underfoot." We, on the other hand, remember all too well the guilt of our brother, and in a strange way, find delight — or at least relief — in holding onto resentment. So, what are we to do? After all, who is there like God? Do you know what? *We* are like God. No, we are not gods ourselves, of course. But we *are* made in God's "likeness." Which means we can always try to be *like* him! Will we fail? Undoubtedly. Should we keep trying anyway? A wholehearted *yes*!

It is true, sometimes our feelings are just *there*. Sometimes triggers come up and we have to start the whole agonizing process of letting go all over again, just when we thought we'd had it beat. Sometimes unwanted thoughts enter in, and we forget we are not supposed to be going down that road. But none of that determines how merciful we have managed to become, because the only thing that matters is that we pick ourselves back up and try again. That is why Jesus loved his little tax collectors and sinners so very much. They knew they were utterly incapable of following those 613 laws and were totally willing to come to Jesus for help. They acknowledged that they could not do it alone; they knew they needed a Savior. And their humility veritably melted their Savior's heart.

Not according to our sins does he deal with us …

THIRD SUNDAY OF LENT

EX 17:3-7; PS 95:1-2, 6-9; ROM 5:1-2, 5-8; JN 4:5-42 (YEAR A)
EX 20:1-17; PS 19: 8-11; 1 COR 1: 22-25; JN 2: 13-25 (YEAR B)
EX 3:1-8, 13-15; PS 103: 1-4, 6-8, 11; 1 COR 10: 1-6, 10-12; LK 13:1-9 (YEAR C)

I am the LORD your God . . . you shall not have other gods beside me.

Few would argue that murder, cheating, lying, and stealing are all reprehensible, even punishable crimes. And yet these commandments are listed *after* a number of other ones — ironically, the ones which many of us do not take seriously at all. "You shall not have strange gods before me," "You shall not take the name of the Lord your God in vain," and "Remember to keep holy the Lord's Day" are prioritized on the list, at least in terms of order, and yet these are the commandments many of us give but a cursory thought to. Let us examine them now, that we might better understand just how seriously God means for us to take them.

You shall not take the name of the LORD, your God, in vain.

Wow. How do we live out this commandment when the expression, "Oh my God" is a part of the everyday vernacular in our culture? Will it really help others to rectify their language if we wag our finger in judgement at them? How do we remain loyal to this commandment without making others feel judged by us? The reality is, most of our friends and family members are likely quite aware how we feel about our faith; we don't have to point out the Ten Commandments for them to know where we stand. So what can we do? We can respond with mercy. And in this case, we can do that in two ways. One, we can give good example. The more others are attracted by the way we live our lives, the more they will be likely to imitate the language they hear us use — or not use. Secondly, every time we hear the Lord's name taken in vain, we can pray under our breath, "May the name of Jesus be praised." Or "Jesus, son of the living God, have mercy on me a sinner." In this way, we counteract with consolation the wound that pierces Jesus's heart when he hears his name misused.

The seventh day is the sabbath of the LORD, your God. No work may be done then.

In a world that no longer closes up shop on Sundays, how do we encourage those around us to live out this commandment? Ironically, by putting forth the effort. "Rest" is not the same thing as doing nothing. The kind of rest the Lord speaks of requires effort, but it is the kind of effort that blesses us and the whole family. Getting the kids up and dressed for Mass can be a monumental task, for example, but the reward reaped after years of perseverance is immeasurable. Likewise, sitting down with our children to play a board game takes a lot more energy than plopping them in front of the TV, and yet if I choose the TV option for them so I can go off by myself to enjoy a good book (even a spiritual one), this is not the kind of rest the Lord is asking of me. Our sabbath is holy if our intention is to pour the love of God into our family and neighbor by doing "*whatever* he tells us" (Jn 2:5).

Honor your father and your mother.

Yikes, this is a tough one. Not all of us have a father or mother who is "honorable." It is relatively easy when the parent is a saint on earth … but what if the parent has been a cause of past wounds? Setting aside the case of abuse, in which we are never required to place ourselves in a position of danger, how are we to understand this commandment with regard to parents whose imperfections and failings have been the source of our pain? For those of us who sincerely desire to follow Christ, having feelings of bitterness toward a parent can cause us further grief by the guilt we feel over perceiving ourselves to be "terrible" sons or daughters who carry such resentful feelings in our hearts. Well, praise be to God, he does not judge us by our feelings. He judges us by our *will.* The fact that we desire not to have such feelings is enough to merit God's mercy! Jesus only requires that we *try*, by turning away from those feelings of bitterness the moment they enter in, and turning instead to God immediately for help. He will restore our peace, even if we need to turn to him every hour — every five minutes — sweating with agonized effort along the way. Our feelings can put us through a terrible ordeal … but *our feelings are not what matter.* What matters is that we *recognize* them, *try* to do the merciful thing anyway (and if we fall — again and again — we pick ourselves back up — again and again), and *trust*, by praising and thanking God specifically for that parent, the very vessel leading us to heaven, as we learn to grow in humility and virtue (Father Michael Gaitley, *33 Days to Merciful Love*). Little by little, our feelings will not be a cause of torment for us anymore. The love of God will permeate not only our will, but our genuine feelings as well.

> *For I, the LORD, your God, am … bestowing mercy down to the thousandth generation on the children of those who love me and keep my commandments.*

MONDAY OF THE THIRD WEEK OF LENT

(2 KGS 5:1-15; PS 42:2, 3; 43:3, 4; LK 4:24-30)

... there were many lepers in Israel during the time of Elisha the prophet; yet not one of them was cleansed, but only Naaman the Syrian.

Such were the words of Jesus that incited the people in the synagogue at Nazareth to drive him out of the town, with the intention of "hurl[ing] him down [the hill] headlong." What infuriated them, of course, was what Jesus's message had to say about *them*: "no prophet is accepted in his own native place."

So we know Jesus could perform few miracles in Nazareth because the people there lacked faith in him. Therefore, we can deduce that Naaman was a man of great faith since he was the only leper that God cured during the time of Elisha — right? Not exactly. It is true, Naaman was willing to go to Israel to be cured, but that was likely only because he was desperate and willing to try anything. When it came down to it, he really did not have much faith at all in the ability of the Jewish God to heal him. The moment he was given instructions as to how to obtain healing, the whole thing seemed like a farce, a fairytale, superstitious magic. Can we blame him? "Go dunk yourself seven times" may as well have been "scratch your ear then blow your nose." Any of us would have felt the same as Naaman. It would have all seemed like smoke and mirrors.

Why, then, *did* God heal Naaman? It is true, Naaman did eventually wash himself in the water, but it was likely a "just in case" move on his part, and not the result of any real, deep, solid foundation of faith. No, if God wills to require faith in order to perform his miracles, he certainly wasn't getting it from Naaman.

> *"If only my master would present himself to the prophet in Samaria," she said to her mistress, "he would cure him of his leprosy."*

Ah. Now wait a minute. Here we *do* see someone who did indeed have faith, the kind with a deep and solid enough foundation to move mountains. Let's remember the servant girl of Naaman's wife is a *slave*, captured by the Arameans "in a raid on the land of Israel." No matter how much she has grown to love her mistress, what that girl had been through must have been both terrifying and traumatizing, having been ripped away from the family she loved and the only world she ever knew. What's more, she'd seen for herself what the people of Aram were capable of. So for her to speak up, would have required on her part either an enormous amount of courage, or an enormous amount of *faith.* Scripture tells us she was a "little" girl, so we can assume it was the latter. This little girl had *certainty* and *sure knowledge* that her God would cure Naaman. Not one ounce of her doubted or simply "wished" it would come true. Her eyes could see what most of us cannot: "the realization of what is hoped for and evidence of things not seen" (Heb 11:1).

> *Naaman went and told his lord just what the slave girl from the land of Israel had said "Go," said the king of Aram. "I will send along a letter to the king of Israel."*

The slave girl was not the only one who had sure faith in the God of Israel. Like Naaman, the King of Aram would have done anything for his "highly esteemed and respected" army commander to be healed. But his desire went beyond wishful thinking and into the realm of certainty, much like the certainty of the slave girl. How do we know this? Scripture tells us that when Naaman tells the King what this "little girl" who has been "captured in a raid" by his own army has said, there is no hesitancy on the part of the King whatsoever. No doubts, no "let me think about it," no questions at all. "Go!" he says. Now let's stop here for a moment, because while we could chalk this up to an overeager, impulsive personality, let's remember this is a *king*, one who is in the habit of raiding and conquering foreign lands and stealing prisoners as slaves; more specifically, little children. This was no softie; it is likely he was more like Attila the Hun! So we can imagine that in all that attacking and raiding, he might have been suspicious of foreigners; would they try to attack back, reclaim what was rightfully theirs? But not a single question escapes this king's lips as to whether the slave girl might be setting a trap, or even whether she might be making up stories as little children often do. No, mystifyingly, something else is at play here. For reasons beyond our comprehension, this king has faith in a God he does not know.

> *But his servants came up and reasoned with him. "My father," they said, "if the prophet had told you to do something extraordinary, would you not have done it?"*

Finally, if the faith of the slave girl was not enough ... if the faith of the King of Aram was not enough ... we see one last group of people that cinch the deal to obtain from God the healing of Naaman: Naaman's own servants. Naaman has lost whatever little hope he'd had that the God of Israel could cure him. He was willing to try a cure the "usual" way — that is, by prayer and imposition of hands, the way one is "supposed" to have it done — but the introduction of this new, foreign concept of washing in the Jordan seven times was too much for him to understand or accept. Naaman is *done*. It is the faith of his servants that persuades him to try again. It is their *love* — as evidenced by their tender name for him ("my father") — that convinces their master to try again, and thus obtains his healing.

So what do we learn from this? Clearly, *our* faith does matter in obtaining healings and conversions and miracles in the lives of others. In fact, it matters so much that the faith they lack is almost inconsequential. I say "almost" because there is one thing they still must do, and this is where we learn our second lesson from today's readings. They must make an act of the will, despite how they *feel*. And it is here that our faith matters too. Sometimes our friends are "on the fence." Sometimes the Christian faith just does not make sense to them. They want to believe ... but simply do not understand how this can be. Our faith is meant to bring light and encouragement to those whose hope is in danger of being lost. Let us not be afraid to persevere in persuading them of Truth. Let us not give up on them, even when all hope seems lost. Let us love them with the heart of a little child. It is *our* faith and *our* love that will melt the heart of the Father, thereby obtaining the grace of God to come pouring down into *their* lives.

Now I know that there is no God in all the earth, except in Israel.

TUESDAY OF THE THIRD WEEK OF LENT

(DN 3:25, 34-43; PS 25:4-9; MT 18:21-35)

Then in anger his master handed him over to the torturers until he should pay back the whole debt. So will my heavenly Father do to you, unless each of you forgives your brother from your heart.

Yikes. Jesus's parable today offers us a lesson in what "forgive us our trespasses as we forgive those who trespass against us" actually means. If we forgive, the Father will forgive us. If we do not, then neither shall he forgive us. Got it.

The thing is, Jesus's words was not an answer to the question, "What will happen to me if I don't forgive my neighbor?" Rather, it was an answer to Peter's question:

Lord, if my brother sins against me, how often must I forgive him?

It would seem that Jesus's answer to that question should simply be, "always," and leave it at that. But Jesus doesn't just leave it at that. He doesn't *just* reply with his famous response: "seventy-seven times." Why not? Why get into this whole scary parable about the punishment we will receive if we do not "forgive [our] brother from the heart"? Is it to frighten us into submission? Doubtfully. After all, fear of punishment might cause us to "act" with forgiveness, but that's hardly the forgiveness that comes "from the heart" which Jesus is demanding of us. So what is Jesus saying here?

Your ways, O LORD, make known to me; teach me your paths, Guide me in your truth …

By relating this specific parable, Jesus is explaining *why* it is so important to forgive always. Peter's question about numbers ("As many as seven times?") implies that he has a person or two in his life that *repeatedly* offends him. Perhaps it is one of the disciples themselves — after all, he doesn't ask about forgiving enemies; rather, the ones Peter refers to he calls "brother." Maybe this "brother" has continually repeated the cycle of offending Peter, saying he's sorry, but then committing the same offensive behavior all over again. How many times is Peter expected to overlook that? Or maybe it's worse: maybe that brother doesn't see any wrongdoing on his own part at all. Maybe he feels justified in his behavior and doesn't even seek forgiveness from Peter. Is Peter expected to forgive something for which the offender is not even sorry? Or perhaps the offender committed a one-time offense, but it was an offense so big, and Peter's heart was wounded so deeply, that the pain has left a permanent scar. He has forgiven him because Jesus said to, but every time a "memento" comes up to remind him of that past wound, Peter's emotions of anger and resentment are triggered all over again. Must Peter forgive all over again that which he has already forgiven? Yes, yes, and yes.

Now if Jesus had left Peter with just a " seventy-seven times " answer but no ensuing parable, perhaps Peter would have followed the Master's teaching out of obedience, but certainly not "from the heart." There would have been no heart in it at all, just 100% an act of the will. Which is actually the only place we have to start. After all, forgiveness isn't a feeling we can manufacture on our own; it is simply a decision that we will act *as though* we hold nothing against the brother who has wronged us. So how do we go from there to "from the heart"? It is this Jesus explains in his parable:

I forgave you your entire debt because you begged me to. Should you not have had pity on your fellow servant, as I had pity on you?

For Peter, listening to Jesus relate his parable that day, and for the rest of us hearing it now, it is *obvious* how hypocritical and mean-spirited is the behavior of the servant who owed the master. We look at him and say, "he should not have done that." It does not take God handing us a list of Ten Commandments to help us figure that out. Jew or Gentile, Christian or non-Christian alike, would know intuitively that to not display the same mercy that the master has shown the servant is utterly contemptible. So why does Jesus feel the need to point this out to Peter? Because while it's "easy" and "obvious" to recognize unmerciful and contemptible behavior in others, seeing it in ourselves is quite another matter. How often do we struggle with a family member who displays the same, repeated, annoying and offensive behavior towards us? How often are we "shocked" and "scandalized" that they did it "again"? Instead of taking it in stride and as no surprise that they should act the way they always have, we turn to a friend who will support our "side" and commence murmuring about the offender all over again ("Can you believe they did this?"). Now don't get me wrong. It is *hard* to be subject to repeated offenses. And to seek the comfort of a friend who recognizes that we are hurting is understandable. Certainly, there is nothing wrong with seeking support from someone who will help us see the hand of God in our pain when we feel alone and in the dark. But the problem lies in looking only at the behavior of *others* who cause *our* wound. Jesus, in his parable today, is asking us to look at things the other way around. We must strive to recognize our *own* sinfulness, lest we be accused by our neighbor of the very same thing that we accuse them of. *That* is how we move from forgiveness as an act of the will to forgiveness from the heart.

> *... he shows sinners the way. He guides the humble to justice, he teaches the humble his way.*

As we begin to take that humble look inward, the Holy Spirit reveals to us that we have our own issues to contend with, our own repeated behaviors that we tend to overlook but which cause others pain. Bad habits formed over the years, so insidious they're almost involuntary. Complaining, moodiness, passive aggressive comments, little sarcastic remarks, arguing, or otherwise brusque behavior. These can be part and parcel of living in a community, but the reality is, it doesn't have to be this way. It simply takes a humble look inward — *recognizing* one's own personal offenses against others — for transformation to begin. We can do little to change the behavior of others. But we can do *a lot* to change our own. By looking inward, we may just find that the behavior we have been so offended by all along is really not all that different from the behavior we display ourselves.

Part two of looking at things the other way around is that we stop focusing on how much we have been hurt. This is not to deny our pain; that would be a form of false humility and would therefore do nothing to help us learn to forgive from the heart. Rather, let us strive to at least recognize that the one who has hurt us has their own personal wounds too. Not just in theory; let us truly try to understand the pain they experience, the one so deep it's been covered in anger, because anger is much easier to deal with than grief. Let us imagine them as little children, who somehow were left with a huge gap between the love they needed and the love they received. The servant in Jesus's parable never looked past his own self to see that pain in the one who owed him. And it was because of this that he was dealt with by the Father this time with justice, and not with the mercy he had received before.

But with contrite heart and humble spirit let us be received … those who trust in you cannot be put to shame.

WEDNESDAY OF THE THIRD WEEK OF LENT

(DT 4:1, 5-9; PS 147:12-13, 15-16, 19-20; MT 5:17-19)

Amen, I say to you, until heaven and earth pass away, not the smallest letter or the smallest part of a letter will pass from the law, until all things have taken place.

Another seemingly contradictory statement coming out of Jesus's mouth in today's Gospel. Yes, we know he did not "come to abolish ... but to fulfill," and yet, Jesus *does* pick grain on the Sabbath, occasionally grabs lunch without washing his hands, and his disciples are not in the habit of fasting. Now, we'll give him a pass because he *is* God after all (God is entitled to do whatever he wants), but as far as expecting the rest of us to not violate the "smallest part of a letter" of the law or to not "teach others to do the same," Jesus is not exactly setting a great example. How do we reconcile today's Gospel passage with his teaching on the "spirit" of the law versus the "letter" of the law, and that "the whole law" depends on just two commandments — that is, to love God and neighbor?

We reconcile it by understanding the *context* in which Jesus is speaking. Jesus has just finished explaining to an enormous crowd of poor, suffering, and sinful people — that is, the marginalized — that their very spiritual poverty is what makes them the most blessed in heaven. "Blessed are the poor," Jesus tells them. "Those who mourn"... "when they insult you and persecute you and utter every kind of evil against you [falsely]"... Jesus tells ones such as these to "rejoice and be glad" because their "reward will be great in heaven." The people in the crowd that day, each individually drawn to Jesus precisely because this was the one place they would have felt loved and wanted and cherished and dignified ... each one would have been thinking, "*I've* been insulted ... you mean, in the end, I'm consoled?" or "*I'm* in mourning, my heart has been torn in two by the death of my husband, my child ... this pain will turn into joy one day, not in spite of my suffering but *because* of it??" Jesus was telling the crowd there was no longer need to ask "why" or to lament "It's not fair." They were the beloved of God. These were the *true* chosen ones.

One of my children is a particularly natural-born helper. I don't have to ask that one to do chores, it's just in her nature to pitch in. She doesn't think twice about it. A true and rare gift for a mother to behold! So one day I wanted this child to know how special she was, how much I appreciated her help, and how rare a gift it is that helpfulness should come so naturally to a child. Then a strange thing happened. The next time she went to wash the dishes, I noticed she started *complaining*. "Can I have a little help here please? Why are the other kids just sitting there? Don't they see how long I've been at this — me, with all the homework I have to do?" Eesh. What happened to my sweet, helpful child? The most likely explanation is that she was simply mimicking her mother (ahem), but the point is still the same. It is human nature to let a compliment get to our heads. Someone says to us, "Thanks for the help," and we hear, "You're better than the others." And this is what Jesus is warning the crowd against in today's Gospel. He is pointing out that their status as God's special ones does not give them license to think they are above the law that the not-so-special ones were enforcing. It would be Jesus's job to put the law-enforcers in their place, not anyone else's. After all, what made the crowd special was not the fact that this one was poor, that one was lame, the other one a widow. What made them special was the *humility* that resulted from the painful circumstances that God allowed in their lives. If they lost their humility in their new-found knowledge of being special, then the very thing that made them special would, paradoxically, count for nothing.

Therefore, whoever breaks one of the least of these commandments and teaches others to do so will be called least in the Kingdom of heaven.

Friends, we don't get to choose which rules we follow based on what's convenient or what we like. We follow them all because Jesus wants us *humble.* There is really only one way to gain the humility that Jesus desires for us and that's by way of practicing *obedience.* That is why 613 laws may have been a heavy burden to carry, but for the people of Israel, in a strange way, it was a *gift.* Why? Because there was no way everyone was going to like all 613 laws, just like so many of us now do not like all the precepts of our Church today. Those laws would have been *hard* to follow; therefore, following them faithfully in obedience would have really meant something to Our Lord. Now maybe when we think of people who have trouble following the rules today, we think of "those" people who skip Mass on Sunday ... the others who see no need to confess their sins to a priest ... the unmarried couples who live together ... all challenging enough to speak against in a society where all such choices have become perfectly acceptable and even expected. But what about us? Do we "like" everything the Church has to say, especially in recent years? Do we welcome the marginalized into our "field hospital for sinners," as Pope Francis suggests, or do we exclude them from a Church we believe to be a "museum" for saints? Perhaps in this time of mercy, Jesus is stirring the pot a little. Because the reality is, we have grown to love the rules we have already been following! Going to Mass on Sunday is not difficult for a person who chooses to go every day. But what happens when we end up on the same playing field as the others who do not like or understand the rules? Will we still follow cheerfully? Or like my child ... will we begin to complain? Jesus is very clear: if we teach others to "do the same" by our complaints or our example of defiance of those in legitimate authority to us, we will end up being "called least in the kingdom." Can you imagine Jesus pointing at us and saying, "You are least"? "Least" on earth translates into humble, but "least" in heaven means we did the minimum required, but not our best. It means we could have done better when we had the chance. Friends, let's practice that "better" way now, while we still *do* have the chance! If there are things we don't like or don't understand from those in legitimate authority to us, giving us legitimate instruction ... *hallelujah*! It is a sure sign to us that Jesus is stretching our capacity to love him. Let us put that love into practice today by doing … whatever he tells us.

> *But whoever obeys and teaches these commandments will be called greatest in the Kingdom of heaven.*

THURSDAY OF THE THIRD WEEK OF LENT

(JER 7:23-28; PS 95:1-2, 6-9; LK 11:14-23)

Faithfulness has disappeared; the word itself is banished from their speech.

What made the generations that came after the time of Moses turn their backs on the faith of their fathers? Their ancestors were enslaved for 400 years and finally set free; they received warning after warning from the prophets to repent from their evil ways ... and neither the knowledge of their people's history nor the admonitions of the prophets were enough to get them to turn their faces once again to God. What made them so hard of heart? Why did they not cherish the gift of faith for which they were the chosen people?

When the terrorist attacks occurred on American soil on September 11, 2001, U.S. citizens were able to witness the event with their own eyes, thanks to televised broadcasting. Just like the attack at Pearl Harbor, Americans woke up to the fact that, for the first time in our generation, our country was not impenetrable. Virtually every American was shaken to the core. The eerie feeling of looking up to a sky void of all aircraft, and the unsettling realization of just how unsafe our lives had become, made us profoundly aware that we did not have control over the uncontrollable. And for a time, churches were full again. The people had awakened to their utter need for a God who would look after them and take care of their lives. We understood like we had never understood before that if we don't turn to God, we will have no way to look after ourselves.

That lasted about three weeks. Then ... eh. Church started to feel boring, praying did not seem to be doing much anyway, resolution was taking too long. So, for most Americans, life returned to the sleepy distraction of football games, restaurants, movies, beer. Life is hard; entertainment is easy — no effort required at all. One does not have to *think* when entertained; one can simply enjoy. Thinking about suffering and death and war and the future is all so ... *unpleasant.* Amusement that we can have now, on the other hand, is not. So that is often where our faces will turn.

Now, let's be clear: it's not an either/or. God does not ask us to deprive ourselves of all joys in life in order to be faithful. After all, life *is* hard, and without those breaks to recuperate, we would be hard pressed to make it through. God is the one who commanded that we take one day a week to rest and enjoy! He *knows* we need our little pleasures in life, and he does not forbid us from looking forward to them: special meals, family vacations, couples' getaways ... God can even use a football game to unite an entire country in prayer! It's just that, when those things become our god, when we make pleasure the idol for which we live and work, then we effectively turn our back on him. We "cannot serve God and mammon" (Mt 6:24).

Whoever is not with me is against me, and whoever does not gather with me scatters.

And herein lies the answer to the "why" question we so often ask when we are undergoing a trial. When we suffer, especially if that suffering is exceedingly difficult, it is human nature to think, "It's not fair." But that is because we have a collective misconception that the easier and more comfortable our lives are, the "luckier" we will be. How often do we hear, "I want to die peacefully in my sleep at the ripe old age of 85?" Who would ever hope to die young after a long and painful illness? Actually ... a few of the saints did! At least, they hoped to suffer valiantly and die martyrs. Now if this makes them sound crazy, understanding their point of view will help us comprehend why they would choose to wear hairshirts throughout their lives, live alone in a cave, or walk over hot coals. They did not do these things because they "enjoyed" pain; they voluntarily took suffering upon themselves so they would be ever aware of their need for God! It is suffering that reminds us of our spiritual poverty, and it is for *this* reason that the God who *could* shield us from it, sometimes chooses not to. When we think, "How could a good God allow us such suffering?"... let's understand that his divine providence always begins and ends with love.

Of course, there are times when perfectly faithful people are made to suffer. Their faces already were turned to God; they did not need a trial to remind them of the God they already worshipped with their whole hearts. Why, then, does God permit suffering in the lives of ones such as these? Because perhaps their suffering is not intended to convert *them.* Perhaps that suffering is intended for someone else. Someone who, thanks to another soul's suffering lovingly offered for their transformation of heart, has picked up a set of rosary beads for the first time in their lives. The suffering of the faithful is never wasted. Every ounce offered is a prayer without ceasing for others to discover the same faith they have.

In my mother's final days of her life, she suffered pain beyond anything she had ever previously experienced. After her passing, someone asked me, "Was it a peaceful death?" I answered, "No, she was in agony." The poor woman did not know how to respond to me! But the reality is, it was my mother's very suffering that brought me peace after she died. You see, my mom was a devout, good, and faithful woman. But perfect? None of us are. But I knew in my heart that whatever vestiges of impurity may have been left in her soul were surely purified in those last days of the purgatory she experienced here on earth. The way I saw it, thanks to her intercession, souls were being saved, and her own soul was now in utter, indescribable, glorious joy ... and my soul too was at peace.

Still ... that kind of suffering is terrifying. The reality is, I am not a particularly courageous soul that can handle intense penances and long, painful illnesses. I want to stay close to God and all, and I certainly pray for the conversion of my loved ones, but I am not ready to say, "Bring it on!" When it comes to huge sacrifices, I am pretty timid. Mercifully, mercifully, Scripture tells us there is one other way to remain faithful to God, to not forget our covenant with him, so that we do not have to take on a grueling penance. It is a hidden door, an escape route from the hard way, and the best-kept secret of our faith. Anyone want in?

Praise and thanks. Praise and thanks. Praise and thanks.

Thanksgiving and praise beget us *immediate* entry into the presence of God, and keep us continually aware that everything we have, we owe to him. It keeps us spiritually poor, even in the midst of pleasure! This. Is. Fantastic. But, of course, there is one tiny catch. Just because praise and thanksgiving keep us from *requiring* suffering to remind us of our need for God, does not mean God won't sometimes send it. But why? Let's remember, as we said earlier, that the suffering we endure is not always meant for our own conversion. It is for the conversion of the souls we pray for too. And from the perspective of eternity, if a mother could see that it was her illness that procured the grace to convert her adult child's heart, she would do it all over again, and more.

So how does praise and thanks help us personally if it won't necessarily prevent us from being recipients of the trials that God sometimes sends? What difference does it make? It makes *all* the difference. You see, weak and little souls don't do too well with suffering — even small ones. Once I twisted my wrist and lay on my recliner, moaning for days in self-pity. "Heaven help us if you actually ever *break* your wrist!" my husband said. So we little ones can't handle very much. But if we prepare for our trials *before* they come, then we will be able to see the hand of God in them. That is what praise and thanks beget us: the grace to *see*. Oh, we may still moan on our recliner ... but we're not asking "Why," and we're not saying, "It's not fair." The only thing that escapes our lips is "Thank you." And we really mean it! There is a genuine sweetness in our suffering (dare I say joy?), because from the bottom of our hearts we *know* that God would never allow our trials if he did not intend to draw something good out of them. And we cannot wait to see what's coming! The soul who practices praise and thanks is full of *hope*. Her presence encourages those around her, though she herself might be in the most pain of all. For her, faithfulness has not disappeared at all; she is the one who brings it back — to her entire generation! So let us praise and thank God today — for everything! Let us sing hymns with joy that a shower of grace might fall upon our families, our Church, our nation ... and our entire generation!

> *We know that all things work for good for those who love God, who are called according to his purpose.* (Rom 8:28)

FRIDAY OF THE THIRD WEEK OF LENT

(HOS 14:2-10; PS 81:6-11, 14, 17; MK 12:28-34)

Unseen, I answered you in thunder…

It is one of the greatest mysteries of God the Father, that he should will to communicate his existence to us through his word, through what we can hear, through the divine voice which we listen to ... and not through what we can *see*; that is to say, his *face*. Often people who struggle with doubt use as the very evidence for their skepticism the fact that no one has physically seen God. How do we know people aren't making stuff up, that religion isn't a form of wishful thinking to combat the frightening alternative about what happens after we die? The thing is, regardless of seeing or hearing, someone who willfully chooses to persist in doubt will never come to accept, because it is not simply a matter of what we can see or what we can hear that enables us to understand; it is a matter of what we *believe*.

For we walk by faith, not by sight … (2 Cor 5:7)

Now if that sounds no different than a child who is convinced that a man in a red suit comes down his chimney delivering bicycles and board games once a year, the difference is this: whereas the child has only the tale of others to take at face value, but no way to gather evidence, we have both the faith that has been passed down the generations, *and* a way to see for ourselves. A blind person does not "believe" in sight simply because other people say it exists. He has a sense of it himself because of the evidence he receives from what he can *hear*: birds chirping on a warm spring day, the sound of waves washing up on shore at the beach in summertime, the crunching of leaves under one's feet in autumn, the howling of the wind during a winter storm. All these enable that blind man to "see." God has given us the gift of his *voice*, and if we do not hear it, it is not because he isn't speaking. It is because we are not *listening*.

I am the Lord your God: hear my voice.

Now to "listen" in the spiritual sense means something a little different than it does in the physical sense. Yes, it means to be attentive to the voice of the one speaking, just like it does if I were to "listen" to you. And it also means to take heed and obey, just as it does for the child who "listens" to her parent or teacher. But there's a third aspect to spiritual listening that does not apply in the physical sense, and it is this we must explore if we want to understand how it was so easy for the ancient Israelites to turn their faces away from God, and so easy for our world to do the same today. Many of us simply do not know *how* to listen.

And when Jesus saw that he answered with understanding, he said to him, "You are not far from the Kingdom of God."

There are a few steps we must follow if we want to learn to hear the voice of God, most of them very basic, very simple ... and yet often we don't follow these basic, simple steps, because, like Naaman who scoffed when given simple instructions to obtain healing, the instructions we're given seem to us *too* basic and simple. It may even seem like we've "already tried that." So let's look at these steps a little more closely, and see if we can both fine-tune our own hearing, as well as help others to recognize the voice of God they have never known.

The first step in being able to hear God's voice is that we must enter into his presence. Yup, that's right, the usual: praise and thanks. (If that seems to be the answer for everything, well, it actually *is*). Thanking God for the good things he gives us is a rare attribute these days; most of the time we forget just how desperate we were to receive the thing five minutes before it was ours. The unknown was almost more than we could bear, the thoughts of "if only" oppressing us ... but then what happens once things go the way we'd hoped? Off we go our merry way, forgetting that things could have easily gone in the opposite direction. Like the nine lepers whom Jesus cured, we take what he gives us without a word of appreciation. In this digital age, many kids today are no longer taught the long-lost art of mailing thank you notes (they don't even know how to properly address an envelope!). And it is a shame. Because as much as thank you notes can put a smile on the recipient's face, that thank you note has the much more important purpose of teaching children to be *grateful.* Instructing kids to say "thank you" is not just about ingraining in them polite manners. It is training them to enter into the presence of God.

Now the thing about "thank you" is that while a contingent of us are poorly educated in the art of showing appreciation for gifts, many of us are not. We are good at sending thank you notes, we've been raised to always express our appreciation for courtesies and compliments received from other people. And when something joyful or exciting happens, the first words out of our lips are, "Thank you, Jesus!" And certainly, Jesus is both happy at our giddiness, as well as pleased by our joy. He rejoices with us! But when good things happen to us, this is generally not the time when we bemoan not being able to hear God's voice. During the times when it seems God has answered our prayers exactly as we were hoping he would, our faith, if anything, gets a "boost." It is during the times when life stinks that we call our ability to hear him into question. And herein lies the crux of why the "basic" and the "simple" become not so obvious anymore. Because in order to trust, we must learn to thank God not just for the things we like, but also for the things we *don't.* Well, who on earth would want to do that? Absolutely no one. Which is precisely why that kind of gratitude is such a powerful act of trust. Saying "thank you" for the things we don't like is the same as telling God we have *certain* confidence that he is taking care of us, that he has a plan, and that he would never allow us our suffering unless he intended to draw a greater good out of it. If thanking God for the things we like enters us into his presence, then thanking him for the things we don't sits us right up on his lap.

But then what? After all, when we're suffering, that's when it's *hardest* to pray. We can't think, we can't read, we can't speak. It seems that all we can do is just sit. Which is painful ... but also *brilliant.*

Be still and know that I am God. (Ps 46:10)

"Sitting there" and "doing nothing" is precisely what brings us to step two: silencing our exterior so that our interior can receive his word. Prayer is nothing more than a communication of hearts, and in the speech of the Spirit, no words are necessary, nor can they adequately encompass what the Father has to say to us. The only word the Lord has to communicate to us, in the end, is *love*, and it is through suffering that our hearts stretch and expand in a capacity to love like they never have before.

Hear, O Israel! The Lord our God is Lord alone! You shall love the Lord your God with all your heart, with all your soul, with all your mind, and with all your strength. The second is this: You shall love your neighbor as yourself.

Now praise and thanks and prayer are all ways we learn to listen to the voice of God, but there is also another very basic, very simple, very obvious way to hear his voice ... so simple and obvious, in fact, that it seems like it wouldn't "work." The family Bible has collected dust on our nightstands generation after generation, with the mistaken belief that what's in there is a bunch of exaggerated stories written by an ancient people long ago. Yes, most Christians believe there was a Jesus, and even accept that he is the Son of God … but what purpose is there in reading the at-times confusing stories of his life, ones we have already heard a thousand times before at Mass? The point is this: "the word of God is living and effective, sharper than any two-edged sword, penetrating even between soul and spirit, joints and marrow, and able to discern reflections and thoughts of the heart" (Heb 4:12). In other words, Scripture does not just tell us the story of what happened *then*; it tells us what is happening *now*. The historical account of what happened in the past is the part that may seem to us as though we've heard it "a thousand times before," but the story of what is happening now is ever fresh and ever current, and so every time we read the very same words, our Father in heaven will teach us something *new*. The account of Jesus's life will then come alive for us; we will pick up details we could have sworn we'd never heard before; and it will teach us something about how to handle our own personal difficulties, how to live our lives *now*. We will find that Scripture really is the only reading we ever need, as it was for St. Therese of Lisieux. We simply need to dust off that Bible and pick it up. It really is that basic.

> *Let him who is wise understand these things; let him who is prudent know them.*

Finally, once we have learned to listen to the voice of God by entering into his presence with praise and thanks, seeking him in the silence of our hearts, and hearing his tangible word in the Scriptures ... after a while, we just kind of know what our Papa sounds like. We recognize his voice, just like sheep who recognize the voice of their shepherd. Our Shepherd has one utterly distinguishing characteristic to his voice: it restores peace to our hearts, even when his words may be hard for us to hear. The Shepherd's voice encourages us and uplifts us, even in the midst of troubling circumstances. And when we can learn to recognize his voice in prayer and the Scriptures, we begin to learn to recognize it in *everything*: in the books we read, in the programs we watch, in the friends — and the not-our-friends — who speak to us. We learn to distinguish who is his messenger from who is not by the measure of peace with which their words fill us. Not a false sense of peace which denies truth for the sake of compromise, but rather a deep, abiding peace which reminds us that everything that befalls us in life is under the providential care of the Father and will therefore work for good in the end. In the words of St. Teresa of Avila, we truly "let nothing disturb" us, when we remain in God's word.

> *Have no anxiety at all, but in everything … with thanksgiving, make your requests known to God. Then the peace of God that surpasses all understanding will guard your hearts and minds in Christ Jesus.* (Phil 4:6-7)

SATURDAY OF THE THIRD WEEK OF LENT

(HOS 6:1-6; PS 51:3-4, 18-21; LK 18:9-14)

Jesus addressed this parable to those who were convinced of their own righteousness and despised everyone else.

We all know well the parable of the Pharisee and the tax-collector. Jesus uses the image of a tax-collector to represent any sinner with true humility and contrition in his heart, and he uses the image of the Pharisee to represent ... well, the very Pharisees who would have been listening to him that day. It was a pretty thinly disguised analogy, likely so there would be no mistake as to whom exactly Jesus was referring. So it is to these that Jesus addresses this parable: the Pharisees who were "convinced of their own righteousness." The thing is ... to say that they were not only "convinced of their own righteousness" but also that they "despised everyone else" is a bit of an overstatement, isn't it? Just because I think I am right about something doesn't mean I despise the person who I think is wrong, after all. I may even love them! Lucy and Ricky Riccardo were the quintessential bickering TV couple, but nobody entertained by those black and white reruns believed their disagreements to be grounds for divorce.

Of course, TV is not real life, and though a married couple can have genuine feelings of affection for each other and still bicker, according to Jesus, to act this way is to act without love. We cannot take a position of self-righteousness and claim to love at the same time. No matter how much our hearts flutter in the presence of another, Christian love is negated by self-righteousness, because Christian love is not a feeling, but rather an act of the will. Thus, it is not an overstatement at all to say that "those who were convinced of their own righteousness" were the same as those who "despised everyone else." Self-righteousness, in the Christian sense, necessarily means that we not only lack love, but that we willfully *despise*. Let's think about that the next time we quibble with our neighbor.

Well, that is enough to scare us off from ever expressing a difference of opinion about anything! Does Jesus intend for us to keep our mouths shut in the face of wrongs, and to not speak out against injustices? Of course not. As Christians, we are called to defend the defenseless, protect the vulnerable, stand up for the ones who cannot stand up for themselves. As a matter of fact, that happens to be one of the built-in jobs that comes with being a parent! What, then, is Jesus suggesting we do?

For it is love that I desire ... and knowledge of God ...

What Jesus asks us to do is to take a humble look inward *first* before we become convinced of our own self-righteousness. When couples bicker — or when anyone bickers over differences of opinion for that matter — most of the time, it stems from a total lack understanding of the other's point of view. We look only through the lens of our own perspective, which is therefore generally *wrong*. Why should it be wrong? Because *our* point of view is tainted by our wounds, past mistakes, hardness of heart, and general lack of knowledge over details of circumstances we are simply not privy to. "But what about them?" we ask. "They did this. They said that. They are the ones who are clearly wrong!" Maybe. But we have absolutely no way of knowing from *our own point of view*. That is not to say *their* point of view is necessarily correct either. But there is one point of view that is always, always objectively correct, 100% of the time: the point of view of the Lord.

Let us know, let us strive to know the LORD...

It is only by asking the Lord, "How do *You* see this?" that our self-righteousness will give way to a view which is *actual* righteousness. So how do we know for sure the righteousness we think we now see is indeed of God, and not tainted by our own thinking or desire or imagination? The very first and surest sign to us that it is God pointing out the truth is that what we see most clearly and distinctly — far surpassing the wrongdoing of our neighbor — is the shameful and sinful ways *we* have contributed to the problem. Our eyes become open to the times we poked a festering wound ... the caustic words we did not hold back ... the times we refused to forgive ... the resentment we hold onto now. Pretty soon, we find it hard to remember what that neighbor even did to cause such anger inside us ... or if we can remember, we can now see all too well that we too do not "deserve" to be forgiven by them. And now, every time a new hurt comes up that pokes the memory of our old one, we sense the Lord pointing out to us that our behavior is not much different than theirs.

> *But the tax collector stood off at a distance and would not even raise his eyes to heaven but beat his breast and prayed, "O God, be merciful to me a sinner."*

As we beat our breast in sorrow, we are now in a disposition to view the divisions we have with our neighbor through a new set of eyes. It's not that they're "bad" and we're "good;" it's that we're both just *broken.* So how can we help fix it? It is from *this* perspective that Jesus wishes us to address the wrongdoing. *This* is how we truly love the neighbor who has failed to love us back. We see the picture from the perspective of eternity, one that looks at the wound and seeks to heal it with a soothing balm of peace. There may indeed come a time we need to correct, to reprimand, to warn, and even to "shake the dust from our feet" as we walk away (Mk 6:10). However, none of that is to be done out of self-righteousness, but rather, in the bond of peace. We have let the "peace of Christ control our hearts," and now "the word of Christ dwell[s] in [us] richly."

> *Put on then, as God's chosen ones, holy and beloved, heartfelt compassion, kindness, humility, gentleness, and patience, bearing with one another and forgiving one another... And over all these put on love, that is, the bond of*

perfection. And let the peace of Christ control your hearts, the peace into which you were also called in one body. And be thankful. Let the word of Christ dwell in you richly… singing psalms, hymns, and spiritual songs with gratitude in your hearts to God. (Col 3:12-16)

FOURTH SUNDAY OF LENT

1 SM 16:1B, 6-7, 10-13; PS 23: 1-6; EPH 5:8-14; JN 9:1-41 (YEAR A)
2 CHR 36:14-16, 19-23; PS 137: 1-6; EPH 2: 4-10; JN 3: 14-21 (YEAR B)
JOS 5:9-12; PS 34:2-7; 2 COR 5: 17-21; LK 15: 1-3, 11-32 (YEAR C)

So some of the Pharisees said, "This man is not from God, because he does not keep the sabbath." But others said, "How can a sinful man do such signs?" And there was a division among them.

The Pharisees are perhaps best remembered in the Christian community for their blind pride, their jealousy, and their hypocrisy, but what we ought to understand about the Pharisees is that they were the keepers of the faith. They could not allow false teaching to enter into their sacred tradition, and therefore anyone making claims of divine healing would absolutely be put to the test. In fact, they would be put to exceedingly *stringent* tests. We need our keepers of the faith because the alternative, in our desperation to be healed, is to follow every "prophet" under the sun who claims to have tapped into the power of the Holy Spirit. My mother suffered a lot of pain in her lifetime and was willing to try *anything* to relieve it. I remember my dad handling a jar of bees once because my parents were told it was a treatment for rheumatoid arthritis. I don't know if it is or if it isn't, but I do know that if my mom was willing to have her back lanced again and again by the stinger of a bee, her pain had to be unimaginable. (She never did get any better from all those bee stings).

So the Pharisees wanted to make sure Jesus wasn't a fraud,

peddling bee stings for sale. And there was nothing wrong with that intention; protecting the faith is a *good* thing. But the problem was not that they had questions for him, but rather, that they were not open to any other answer than the one they had already predetermined in their minds. The problem was not that the Pharisees wanted to be sure; the problem was they wanted to be *right.*

> *"You were born totally in sin, and are you trying to teach us?" Then they threw him out.*

In many ways we are just like those Pharisees; we can understand them. We too have a conviction about our faith, unwilling to compromise with that which we are sure is true. So what can we do to ensure our conviction doesn't translate into the same hardness of heart as that of the Pharisees? How do we remain "keepers of the faith," but at the same time, have hearts that remain open to the "new wineskins" that Jesus offers us? St. Paul tells us there is a way:

> ... *everything exposed by the light becomes visible, for everything that becomes visible is light.*

We must start by taking that humble look inward and acknowledging our own sins before we can discern what is right and true in others. What happens when our own inner weakness and imperfection is exposed to the light and becomes visible? According to St. Paul, those imperfections and weaknesses become themselves the very light by which we can *see*:

> ... *light produces every kind of goodness and righteousness and truth.*

So the first step in doing "what is pleasing to the Lord" is acknowledging and confessing our sins. What more must we do?

> *For by grace you have been saved through faith, and this is not from you; it is the gift of God; it is not from works, so no one may boast.*

Jesus indeed has given each of us some beautiful graces, there is no doubt about it. But the moment we think they are "ours," is the moment that whatever fruit which comes forth from our gift will turn rotten.

I love writing. Years ago, someone suggested I journal in front of the Blessed Sacrament to jot down what I felt the Lord speak to my heart. It was wonderful! But pretty soon I was journaling all the time … and eventually I would sit down to journal without praying, because it would all come so … easily. Over time I realized that as beautiful as much of what I wrote sounded, there was one or two things that seemed "off." It took some time, and some hard lessons along the way, but eventually I knew in my heart that what I had spent so much time writing was not of God. Perhaps some of it might have been biblically sound, but I had no way of sorting through what was and what was not. All I knew was that if a small part of it had been tainted by a spirit that was not divine, then I did not want any of it. I threw in the garbage all those journals which at one point I had consulted for guidance. It was definitely a humbling experience. A Christian's whole life should branch out from the Lord's vine. We must decrease so that he may increase. Like St. Paul, we must learn to be *humble.*

> *Blessed is the man who perseveres in temptation, for when he has been proved he will receive the crown of life.* (Jas 1:12)

Now, learning to be humble does not require us to endure continual and miserable humiliations and suffering every moment of every day for the rest of our lives. But if we want to imitate St. Paul, who imitated Christ, then we must *accept* whatever befalls us with *peace.* A Christian is not frazzled, anxious, afraid, or angry by adverse circumstances that come his way. When others are around us, they should have a sense that everything is going to be ok, even when there is a lot on our plate. We remain peaceful and cheerful because we can see the hand of God working in our lives, and we can point out his hand to others in their own lives too. We are detached from outcomes, because we want only that which God wants, which necessarily will always be for the best. A Christian *trusts.*

> … *if it dies, it produces much fruit.* (Jn 12:24)

Paul gave his life for the ones who came into his path, rich or poor, slave or free, Gentile or Jew. Like St. Paul, we do not act one way with some people, another way with others. A Christian is not a hypocrite. We love the ones we do not like as if they were our very own children. We do not give preferential treatment to anyone, nor do we snub, shun, or avoid those whom the Lord has sent into our lives who happen to drive us crazy. We strive to see the face of Jesus in every face we encounter; we beg Jesus for that grace at the start of each day.

But whoever lives the truth comes to the light, so that his works may be clearly seen as done by God.

Finally, others should know we are Christians by our love (Jn 13:35). Let's make sure our minds are not "occupied with earthly things" by making it not about our disagreements, but about the souls with whom we disagree. Let's look at their wound and not at their behavior, and in so doing, elicit the grace of mercy in our hearts.

God was entrusting the world to himself in Christ, not counting their trespasses against them and entrusting to us the message of reconciliation.

MONDAY OF THE FOURTH WEEK OF LENT

(2 SM 7:4-5, 12-14, 16; PS 89:2-5, 27, 29; ROM 4:13, 16-18, 22; MT 1:16, 18-21, 24; LK 2:41-51)

Go, tell my servant David, "When your time comes and you rest with your ancestors, I will raise up your heir after you, sprung from your loins ... And I will make his royal throne firm forever. I will be a father to him, and he shall be a son to me."

Of course, we all know the heir that has "sprung" from the "loins" of David to whom the Lord refers is Jesus Christ himself. Except that ... Jesus did not *actually* "spring" from David's "loins." As a matter of fact, there were no loins involved in his conception at all. So why does Scripture phrase his genealogy in such a *specific* way, only to expect humanity to later accept that Jesus was conceived by the Holy Spirit? Couldn't there have been another way to word this sacred prophecy so that it would not appear to be such a contradiction later, and frankly, so that it would be an easier pill to swallow when the time came?

Behold, this child is destined for the fall and rise of many in Israel, and to be a sign that will be contradicted ... (Lk 2:34)

It appears that Jesus's birth was intended by God to be "contradicted." But to what end? Why make the circumstances surrounding his birth such an obstacle to belief? Simeon's prophecy offers a pretty clear answer to that question:

> .... *so that the thoughts of many hearts may be revealed.* (Lk 2:35)

In other words, to come to accept that Jesus was "sprung from the loins" of David, while at the same time not the biological son of Joseph, would never happen by way of reasoning, proof, or otherwise convincing arguments. There would be only one way for the Israelites to accept this seemingly contradictory prophecy: that is, by way of *faith*. That is why Jesus, from the moment of his conception, was a sign that "revealed the thoughts of many hearts." Those who accepted the sprung-from-the-loins-of-David-but-conceived-by-the-Holy-Spirit contradiction accepted such a proposal by way of *faith*. Those who did not, viewed Jesus's birth strictly through the lens of human reasoning.

> *[The promise] depends on faith, so that it may be a gift, and the promise may be guaranteed to all his descendants, not to those who only adhere to the law but to those who follow the faith of Abraham, who is the father of all of us.*

Now before we go thinking that those who reason are the "bad guys," and those who believe are the "good guys," let's realize that the ability to reason is not a bad thing. In fact, as a community — as a *nation* — we have spent far too little time using that God-given ability in recent years! Jesus wants us to reason, to think, to use logic. The problem lies in our using the gift of reason to the exclusion of openness to the new wineskins that Jesus offers us.

> "Faith and reason are like two wings on which the human spirit rises to the contemplation of truth." (St. Pope John Paul II, *Fides et Ratio*)

The greatest minds that procured the explosion of scientific discovery that took place during the Renaissance were men and women of incredible intellect, it is true. But most notably, these were men and women of deep *faith*. It seems our modern age has divided faith and reason, which has resulted in the unfortunate consequence of "advances" that have been made not only to our benefit, but to our detriment as well. When faith and reason work in conjunction with each other, the result is always to our benefit alone.

So the Lord doesn't fault us for using our reason. When it comes from a motivation to learn and not from an intention to simply prove that which one has already predetermined, our reason will always inevitably lead us to the truths of our faith, because our faith is the most reasonable truth there is. In the end, faith is the *only* truth that makes any sense at all. As a matter of fact, while we must approach our conclusions through the lens of faith, the Lord never asked us to do so without the gift of our reason, a gift which *he* himself gave us. Without reason and logic, we place ourselves at the risk of believing ... well, everything we hear. We risk believing every conspiracy theory on the internet, every ominous warning from every self-proclaimed prophet, and every person who says, "God said to me ..." All of which may be true. But also ... may *not.* And it is the beliefs that are not true that can jeopardize the very faith that keeps us trusting and open to the things of the Spirit. We must use *both* faith and logic if we want to be obedient and trustworthy followers of Christ. It is the very built-in system of checks and balances that God has placed on every human soul, and it's what separates us from the animals. Let's not forsake the gifts God has given us.

> *Jacob was the father of Joseph, the husband of Mary. Of her was born Jesus who is called the Christ.*

So we understand why faith is required in order to believe that Jesus is both "sprung from the loins" of the line of David, but at the same time is not his biological heir ... but where does the "reason" part come in? After all, there is a very obvious contradiction here which our minds cannot reconcile. Ah! It is here that, according to St. Anselm, our "faith seeks understanding."

> *"Your father and I have been looking for you with great anxiety"... "Did you not know that I must be in my Father's house?" ... But they did not understand what he said to them.*

Mary refers to Joseph as Jesus's "father," though she knows full well Joseph is not his biological father, but rather his foster one.

They both fully accept that Jesus was conceived of the Holy Spirit, that he's the Messiah ... but when Jesus says to them, "Did you not know that I must be in my Father's house?" ... they have no clue what he means. Isn't that odd? They did not say, "Ok, sure, you need time to pray with your Father God in the temple, but we don't understand why you didn't tell us where you were going." Rather, "they did not understand what he said to them." In other words, Joseph and Mary, it would seem, did not as yet think of God as a "father." Jesus has not yet revealed that aspect of the First Person of the Trinity — evidently, not even to his own parents! Further, despite knowing that Jesus was not conceived by way of Joseph's "loins," Mary considered Joseph to be Jesus's father just as much as if Jesus had descended from Joseph's lineage; that is how close the two were. But it is also how close the Father wants to show us that he is to us. Joseph was "foster" father to Jesus, it is true. But the fact that they did not share DNA did not take a single ounce of love away from the familial bond between them. In fact, when God is one of the two people in a relationship, the strength of the bond is even *greater*. American singer Marie Osmond was once asked by a reporter which of her seven kids was adopted. She answered with a big smile, "I can't remember." Any adoptive parent who has experienced the absolute yearning for a child before they receive that baby in their arms — the waiting, the unknowns, the anticipation — understands full well Marie Osmond's words. Love transcends biology. Now why is it important for us to understand this transcendence in Joseph's and Jesus's father/son relationship? Why does God want us to know just how close their relationship was, so much so that Joseph and Mary did not understand when Jesus called God his "father"? Friends, there is just one reason alone. When we are baptized, we become "adoptive" children of God, it is true. But we are his children just as surely as we are the children of the parents from whom we were conceived. In fact, even *more* so. That is how close our adoption makes us to God. The Father doesn't look at us and think, "That's not my *real* baby." The Father looks at us and says: *you are mine* (Is 43:1). And knowing this, do we really think he's going to let us go if we have asked him to "never permit us to be separated from [him]" (*Spiritual Communion Prayer*)? Do we really think he's going to forget if we have a giant problem on our hands, one too big for us to solve on our own? Do we really have to doubt that he watches over us, continually, arranging all things in our lives to bring about the best possible outcome? If our souls were not at peace before, let us finally allow this reasoned truth of our faith sink in. It's really all we need to know.

> *"You are my father, my God, the Rock, my savior." Forever I will maintain my kindness toward him, and my covenant with him stands firm.*

TUESDAY OF THE FOURTH WEEK OF LENT

(EZ 47:1-9, 12; PS 46:2-3, 5-6, 8-9; JN 5:1-16)

Look, you are well; do not sin any more, so that nothing worse may happen to you.

Now wait a minute here. Is Jesus implying here that personal misfortune is a direct result of our sin? Because how we understand the answer to that question will affect how we view our circumstances and the circumstances of others. Therefore, let's clear up any confusion we might have over Jesus's seemingly contradictory words that we might gain clarity and insight into exactly what Our Savior means.

It is true that the Father doesn't send us afflictions like blindness as a way of "punishing" us for our sinfulness. The reality is, we all deserve far worse than that for our offenses against him anyway. When Jesus told the disciples that the blind man's impairment was not the result of his parents' sin (Jn 9:3), he was not suggesting that those parents were perfect, or that they never did anything wrong in their lifetime. As a matter of fact, it is certain that the thought of their personal sin must have crossed their minds; they either wondered what they did that was so bad or attributed their chastisement to a hidden transgression from long ago. They were likely racked with guilt and shame because they would have known that their lives weren't spent without vice, and now the proof of that was evident to all the world. But Jesus points out to the disciples that this is not how God operates. God indeed is the one who sends or allows the afflictions in our lives, but it is always, always with the intention of prompting us to turn our hearts back to him. Just as a mother bird pushes her baby bird out of the nest so that he learns to fly, so too Our Lord sometimes allows us to fall in order that we reach our arms *up* to him.

Still ... in today's Gospel, Jesus tells the man who has been ill for thirty-eight years not to sin "so that nothing worse may happen to you." What could be "worse" than being ignored for thirty-eight years as one lay ill at the side of the Bethesda Pool? Laying ill and ignored for *thirty-nine* years ... or more. In other words, Jesus is telling the man who has been healed that if he returns to his former way of life, so too would his illness return to him. Jesus is saying here that there is a direct correlation. But how do we reconcile this with his words about the blind man, whose blindness, Jesus told the disciples, was not the result of his sin? Is Jesus suggesting that this man's thirty-eight years of illness *was* a direct result of his sin? It is quite possible. You see, while God does not send us afflictions in order to "punish" us, sometimes we do it to ourselves. If I overeat, I will suffer a stomachache. If I drink too much alcohol, I will suffer a hangover. And in the case of the healed man ... we can only speculate as to what he did that was "too much." Perhaps it was simply that he lay on the mat for far too long. After all, Scripture doesn't tell us the man was paralyzed; we hear only that the man was "ill." Perhaps his illness was the sickness of self-pity, keeping him from getting up and walking out of one of those five porticos. We do not know. But it is certain that a fall back into a puddle of self-pity would surely bring him right back to the spot he was in before, only "worse." Worse, because this time he would have known what it would have felt like to be well in the presence of Jesus and would have longed to have that back more than anything. Worse, because this time he would not have the people who did not put him in the pool to blame. This time, he would have no one to blame but himself.

They asked him, "Who is the man who told you, 'Take it up and walk'?" The man who was healed did not know who it was, for Jesus had slipped away, since there was a crowd there.

The fact is, the man healed of his illness doesn't know who it is who healed him ... because Jesus doesn't allow him to know. This is *intentional.* Why Jesus should will to keep him from knowing who he is, we can only speculate. But suffice it to say, there was a period of time that the Pharisees and the other Jews were not as yet meant to find Jesus, and then a definite time that God allowed the persecution to begin. Before God allowed them to find Jesus, Jesus's "time has not yet come" (Jn 2:4).

So what does this mean for us? We all know the experience of someone we love afflicted with something for far too long. Perhaps that someone is even us. Let's realize that if this is the case, then if we've placed our lives — and the lives of those we love — in the hands of God, we can have peace in knowing that this is simply the time *before* the "prescribed" time. There is a period that precedes the definite period of healing, and it is here that sometimes souls need to hit "rock bottom" before turning their lives over to the Lord. Yes, it is awful to witness. Yes, the temptation to ask "why" and to wonder "what if" is so great, it threatens to come over us like a tidal wave, drowning us in a tsunami of self-pity. It is then we must look *up.* Because as menacing as that tsunami is, it is as nothing compared to the *ocean* that is God's mercy! So let's allow that mercy to swallow up our fear. Jesus has given us a weapon at our disposal and though it is tiny, it is *powerful*, and it not only holds back the tidal wave that threatens to crush us, but it also turns that wave into a peaceful swell, a "sea of blessings" (*Diary of St. Faustina*). What is that weapon? *Trust.* So let's use that weapon daily, continually, and forevermore, by giving God praise and thanks in all things. In this way, we will ensure that we carry our mat and carry our cross for the rest of our lives ... but never again carry the affliction of fear.

WEDNESDAY OF THE FOURTH WEEK OF LENT

(IS 49:8-15; PS 145:8-9, 13-14, 17-18; JN 5:17-30)

For this reason they tried all the more to kill him, because he not only broke the sabbath but he also called God his own father, making himself equal to God.

What must this scene have been like? One can almost picture the crowd enraged, shouting, holding torches and pitchforks, chasing after this Jesus who had just, in their view, blasphemed their faith. Making himself equal to God? Sacrilege! And yet ... we do not hear that Jesus "passed through the midst of them" as he'd done before (Lk 4:30), or that he "withdrew to a deserted place" (Mt 14:13), or that he put up his dukes, covered himself with armor and weaponry, or otherwise engaged in battle. No. Instead, Jesus does something rather curious:

Jesus answered and said to them ...

Jesus *answered.* In other words, he responds not to their action but to their *question.* But what question? Any "question" the crowd would have been asking would not have been one that sought true clarity or sincere understanding; their minds were already made up: Jesus must go. So what question could they possibly have been asking in that volatile moment that could have allowed a long enough pause to afford Jesus time to speak? Just one, really.

WHO DO YOU THINK YOU ARE?

It is to this question, whether verbalized or simply formulated in their minds, that Jesus gives one of the clearest and most emphatic answers of his entire earthly ministry:

Amen, amen, I say to you ... just as the Father raises the dead and gives life, so also does the Son give life to whomever he wishes. Nor does the Father judge anyone, but he has given all judgment to the Son, so that all may honor the Son just as they honor the Father.

These Jews, in their anger, have likely asked their question for the purpose of inciting a riot ... and instead, Jesus answers their rhetorical question quite literally. But why? Normally, Jesus tells those looking for proof that "no sign will be given" (Mt 16:4), and he essentially tells those to whom he has previously offered explanation, "I have already told you." So why go into such emphatic and excessive detail now about who he is and what his role for humanity will be? It would seem Jesus does this so there would be no mistake about who exactly it is this crowd was intending to kill, and so they would not later be able to make any excuses that they "didn't know." If they were going to go through with the execution of the Savior, they were going to do it with their eyes wide open.

But surely, they didn't *really* understand? After all, who would ever knowingly kill *God*? Well, my friends, we all would. It's what happens every time we do something that we know is wrong but do it anyway. Sure, maybe our small transgressions pale in comparison to what the crowd did to Jesus ... but that's because Jesus took all sin upon himself and shows us what that sin looks like. When we look at the cross, we see with our own eyes what the sins we commit *now* did to Jesus *then*. Our personal sin can seem so hidden, so minor, that we can convince ourselves it is not really hurting anyone. It is amazing what we can justify to ourselves (*But they hurt me first ... But they don't deserve my forgiveness ... How can I be expected to love someone who acts that way?*). But our justifications, in the end, are not much different from the justifications these Jews made to themselves when they went after Jesus, despite having been told who he was. Jesus allowed them to go after him ... but not before he made clear precisely what their actions would mean. Today, Jesus wants our eyes open too. *Amen, amen,* he says to us.

> *… the Son cannot do anything on his own, but only what he sees the Father doing; for what he does, the Son will do also.*

It's interesting that the crowd tried "all the more" to kill Jesus because he had "ma[de] himself equal to God" by "call[ing] God his own father," and yet the first thing Jesus tells them is that he "cannot do anything on [his] own." He is obviously not making a statement to deny his divinity; after all, he later tells them that God has given him "power to exercise judgment," a power reserved for God alone. And he adds that it is "because he is the Son of Man," a title referring to the Messiah. So why the apparent contradiction? Why does Jesus claim his divinity, while at the same time inform these Jews there is nothing he can do on his own? Can't God do anything and everything?

> *... though he was in the form of God, [he] did not regard equality with God something to be grasped …* (Phil 2:6)

Jesus indeed is the God who can do anything, but the mission for which he was sent is one that *prevents* him from doing that which is not the will of the Father. His mission is one of *humility*. The Father has sent his Son to save us from our sins — the ones we knowingly commit with eyes wide open, no matter how many excuses we make or how much we justify our behavior. But Jesus also came to teach us that his passion, death, and resurrection — all he went through in taking our sins upon himself — will not save us if we do not learn to be *humble*. We do not get an automatic pass to enter heaven, despite everything Jesus went through for us. He is offering us his ticket to the Kingdom, yes, but we still must reach out our hands to receive it. We do that by way of a humble, contrite heart. In this way, our will shall always match the will of the Father too, just as did the will of Jesus. Our will shall ever be to do God's will. And eventually, when we truly want only that which God wants, then we will find that we *always* have what we want! That is why Jesus's statement is no contradiction at all. He was indeed "powerless" to do that which was outside the Father's will, it is true; but that was because Jesus himself willed to be so!

... he humbled himself, becoming obedient to death, even death on a cross. Because of this, God greatly exalted him ... (Phil 2: 8-9)

Part two of the humility Jesus came to teach us is that the only way to obtain such humility of heart that is our ticket to heaven is by way of *obedience.* That's it. Period. "Feeling" humble doesn't cut it because the moment we think we have finally reached true humility of heart, paradoxically, is the moment we have our sure sign that we have not. No, the only way to live humility is by accepting the circumstances that befall us and by following the legitimate commands of those in legitimate authority to us. Sounds awful, right? The thing is ... it is only awful in the beginning of our journey towards humility. Nobody "enjoys" being humiliated, understandably. But after a time, as humility becomes part of who we are, we begin to see things differently. That is, we begin to see the hand of God in our circumstances. Humiliations become offerings. Trials become opportunities to "pray without ceasing." Submission to rules we don't particularly like become ways to love God more. And guess what the byproduct of all that is? A miserable, boring, dark, and depressing life? No way! The byproduct is peace and joy unlike anything we have ever known! How this is possible, to us, is a mystery. The world tells us food + entertainment + fun = happy; but in the spiritual life, fasting + deprivation + solitude = love. Go figure.

He will show him greater works than these, so that you may be amazed.

THURSDAY OF THE FOURTH WEEK OF LENT

(EX 32:7-14; PS 106:19-23; JN 5:31-47)

So the LORD relented in the punishment he had threatened to inflict on his people.

What a strange tale we hear in Exodus today. The Creator of the universe had a plan, but then a mere creature — whose mind God himself fashioned — uses simple logic to "persuade" God to change his plan? First, Moses points out the obvious: that if God made the Egyptians endure locusts and frogs and plague and death in order to set his people free, only to then later slaughter those chosen people in their very place of freedom, the only conclusion that could be drawn by the Egyptians is that the God of Israel had acted with "evil intent" all along. Next, Moses "reminds" the omniscient God of the promise he had made long ago that "all this land" would be a "perpetual heritage" given to the descendants of Abraham, Isaac, and Israel. Well, if God forgot the covenant he himself had made, and if he couldn't see for himself the lack of logic in exterminating the very people he'd worked so hard to set free, then he certainly does not sound like a particularly omniscient God! Of course, the characteristics of not remembering or not reasoning is inconsistent with the God we know. God's wrath is not like human wrath, which flares up suddenly and whose passion and emotion obscure logic and truth. God's wrath is manifested in a divine justice, which remains calm, and, as long as we are still alive, is always intended for the purpose of turning hearts back to the Father; it is one that does not stop pursuing its rescue mission until that lost soul has drawn its last breath. So if Moses didn't really "persuade" God with a superior logic, nor "remind" God of a promise he'd forgotten in his fury ... what role did Moses play in the Lord's relenting of "the punishment he had threatened to inflict on his people"?

> *Then he spoke of exterminating them, but Moses, his chosen one, Withstood him in the breach to turn back his destructive wrath.*

The thing is, the Lord "spoke" to Moses "of exterminating them," but the reality is, such was not his desire. His words to Moses were *intended* to provoke Moses to lay out a defense on behalf of the people. Does this mean Moses' words had no impact on the Lord at all, because God already remembered his covenant with Abraham and had no intention of following through on his threat? Definitely not. Moses absolutely was the instrument who "withstood the beach" and changed the course of history for the Jews. But how? If his logic did not convince God of something he didn't already know, and his reminder did not bring back a memory that God had forgotten, what did his words do to prevent the wrath of punishment that God had threatened to carry out? Moses *interceded.*

> "God wishes our collaboration ... so much that he has made the granting of certain graces, necessary for our salvation and that of others, dependent upon our prayers … [grace] will not be poured out unless there is someone who raises supplicating hands to heaven, asking for it." (Fr. Gabriel of St. Mary Magdalen, *Divine Intimacy*)

It was not Moses' persuasive argument nor his logical reminder that changed the course of events; it was his *prayer* — one that was perfectly in accord with God's very own will. While it is perfectly true that in justice, the people of Israel deserved God's wrath for becoming "depraved" and turning "aside from the way [God] pointed out to them," it is equally true that God's will for them was to receive the grace of *mercy*. As long as they were living and breathing, his will would have been to pour out upon them every spiritual grace that would lead them to repentance. And it is this outpouring of grace upon the entire nation that was dependent upon the prayers of just *one* man. This is *good news* for us! Because the fact is, we can spend an awful lot of time riddled with anxiety over the loved ones in our lives who have "become depraved" or otherwise "turned aside from the way [God] pointed out to them." Much of our effort can be spent in figuring out words that will "remind" them of who they are, or "convince" them to turn back to God, using persuasive arguments and convincing logic. But as we all know too well, our words will fall upon deaf ears if those souls are not first offered the grace that enables them to *hear.* This is why there is no substitute for our prayers on their behalf. These souls *depend* upon them, just as God depends upon us to supply those prayers. And quite frankly … what a relief! Because while we may not come up with the most logical arguments in the world to convince anyone of anything ... we *can* always pray!

Friends, if we have spent most of our time with our wayward loved ones cajoling, coaxing, bargaining, or arguing ... let's table that for today, and simply raise “supplicating hands to heaven.” For today, let's allow Jesus to do the convincing and the reminding. We may very well be exhausted from our seemingly fruitless and endless debating ... but Jesus makes all things new! And if it seems *all* we have been doing is praying ... then for today, let's increase our trust and our confidence in the power of our prayers, the ones the Father depends upon in order to grant those graces that, according to Fr. Gabriel of St. Mary Magdalen, he desires to "pour out abundantly upon men's souls.”

FRIDAY OF THE FOURTH WEEK OF LENT

(WIS 2:1A, 12-22; PS 34:17-21, 23; JN 7:1-2, 10, 25-30)

The wicked said among themselves, thinking not aright: "Let us beset the just one ..."

Today's passage from the Book of Wisdom was written less than one hundred years before the crucifixion of Jesus, so it was a fairly recent prophecy when we consider the whole of salvation history. Still, it was written approximately fifty years before Christ's birth, so no one was extrapolating details from events that were taking place at the time; the author of the book of Wisdom had no link to Jesus whatsoever. And yet ... Wisdom recounts quite possibly the most detailed and specific prophetic account of future events that were yet to take place: "evidence," if you will, that Jesus was indeed the Messiah. Why is this so fascinating? Because most of the time when it comes to biblical prophecy, there is a degree of interpreting and extrapolating going on. Not that the fact that one must extrapolate makes the prophecy inauthentic; it's just that to point to "a bruised reed he shall not break" in the book of Isaiah and then expect the Pharisees to immediately conclude that Jesus is the Messiah ... well, one can understand why it was a bit of a stretch for some. But not so with the Book of Wisdom. The connection should have been both immediate as well as apparent to those well versed in Scripture: the scribes and Pharisees. And yet, these were the first to doubt and condemn. So let's examine this passage a little more closely to see what they missed, and to understand why it was they were loath to accept what should have been obvious to them.

So what did the Pharisees miss?

1. "… he is obnoxious to us …"

You hypocrites! (Lk 12:56)

2. "… he sets himself against our doings …"

... do and observe all things whatsoever they tell you, but do not follow their example. (Mt 23:3)

3. "… [he] reproaches us for transgressions of the law and charges us with violations of our training."

... they preach but they do not practice. They tie up heavy burdens [hard to carry] and lay them on people's shoulders, but they will not lift a finger to move them. All their works are performed to be seen. They widen their phylacteries and lengthen their tassels. They love places of honor at banquets, seats of honor in synagogues, greetings in marketplaces, and the salutation "Rabbi." (Mt 23:3-7)

4. "He professes to have knowledge of God and styles himself a child of the LORD."

I am the way and the truth and the life. No one comes to the Father except through me. (Jn 14:6)

5. "To us he is the censure of our thoughts …"

Jesus knew what they were thinking … (Mt 9:4)

6. "... merely to see him is a hardship for us …"

When the people in the synagogue heard this, they were all filled with fury. (Lk 4:28)

7. "... his life is not like that of others, and different are his

ways."

Why does your teacher eat with tax collectors and sinners? (Mt 9:11)

8. "He judges us debased; he holds aloof from our paths as from things impure."

Woe to you, scribes and Pharisees, you hypocrites ... (Mt 23:13)

9. "He calls blest the destiny of the just ..."

Blessed are the poor in spirit, for theirs is the kingdom of heaven. (Mt 5:3)

10. "... [he] boasts that God is his Father."

So will my heavenly Father do to you, unless each of you forgives his brother from his heart. (Mt 18:35)

11. "Let us see whether his words be true ... With revilement and torture let us put him to the test that we may have proof ..."

They said this to test him, so that they could have some charge to bring against him. (Jn 8:6)

12. "For if the just one be the son of God, he will defend him and deliver him from the hand of his foes ... Let us condemn him to a shameful death; for according to his own words, God will take care of him."

You who would destroy the temple and rebuild it in three days, save yourself, if you are the Son of God, [and] come down from the cross! (Mt 27:40)

Well, the prophetic words about Jesus in the Book of Wisdom could scarcely get more specific. So why did the Pharisees fail to "interpret the present time" (Lk 12:56)?

The first thing we must understand is that while the Book of Wisdom was not part of the Torah, it was a literary manuscript well known by the Jewish leaders. And it would have been respected for its teachings; at the time, it was believed to have been authored by King Solomon himself (although today that is up for debate among theologians). What's more, the proof that the Jewish leaders were well familiar with the writings of Wisdom is that it was quoted by St. Paul (a former Pharisee himself) and alluded to by Matthew in his Gospel. So ignorance of such writings would not have been an acceptable excuse by the Pharisees for not recognizing the prophecy. What, then, was their excuse?

Years ago, one of my teenagers had violated one of our "house rules." She knew it was a violation, so, as teenagers do, she hid the violation from my husband and me. When we found out, of course we were disappointed, and of course there would be a consequence to be meted out; but first, we wanted to understand from her, "What were you thinking?" Our child's response? I could not even tell you. Why? Because *it made no sense.* You see, when we take steps down a path we know from the start is not right ... after a while, we're not so sure about what's right anymore. After all, in the moment of temptation, sin sure "feels" right. It is not until later, after we have already committed the sin, that we feel out of sorts. And if we do not acknowledge in humility that our choice was wrong, if we do not ask for God's forgiveness with a genuine, contrite heart, then we are subject to sin again, no matter how "bad" we felt about ourselves the last time. There is something about willfully engaging in sin that confuses our thoughts. It's not just that we have a difference of opinion with those who do what is right; it's that we cannot see clearly enough to even *know* right from wrong. Persisting in wrong makes our "thinking not aright." And what's more — we don't even realize that we can't see!

> *These were their thoughts, but they erred; for their wickedness blinded them, and they knew not the hidden counsels of God; neither did they count on a recompense of holiness nor discern the innocent souls' reward.*

This pretty much sums up the condition of our world today, doesn't it? There is a definitive lack of understanding between those who hold differences of opinion — and quite frankly, it has little to do with the opinion itself. Our thinking is simply not "aright," and therefore what comes out of our mouths is utter confused nonsense. We say things like, "I don't know how to explain what I'm thinking," or "I'm not eloquent with words," or "I can't argue as well as you can." But to paraphrase Albert Einstein, if we cannot explain our argument to a six-year-old, then we do not understand it ourselves. And we have all had this experience, haven't we? Friends, confusion and lack of logic is a sure sign to us we are walking in a fog; that is, right in the thick of the smoke of Satan.

Well, that's creepy. But lest we lose hope in our ability to discern amidst all the sin and weakness we struggle with ... the Psalms today offers us a word of hope:

The LORD redeems the lives of his servants; no one incurs guilt who takes refuge in him.

Recently I decided to take a hop on the anxiety train and go for a ride. *What if this happens with one of my kids? What if that happens with the other?* It was a path I had not engaged in for quite some time, and I had no idea what I was doing on that train, but I begged the Lord to take me off! Then this morning, I woke up with a quote by Fr. Jacques Philippe in my mind:

"Worry never solved anything; only prayer does."

And boom! I was off the train. What's more, I realized that the whole reason the Lord had allowed me on the train for as long as he did (well, just one day really) is so that I would "take refuge" in him. Yes, I do strive to take refuge in him daily; hopefully we all do. But if Jesus turns the heat up a notch, that is a sure sign to us that he simply wants us to take refuge a little *more*. So if we're undergoing a little "confusion" of our own right now ... in a sense, that is good news. Really good news! Because there is only one way to have our confusion cleared up, and that is by taking "refuge" in him. And friends … refuge in his cloak is the best place to be.

SATURDAY OF THE FOURTH WEEK OF LENT

(JER 11:18-20; PS 7:2-3, 9-12; JN 7:40-53)

But, you, O LORD of hosts, O just Judge, searcher of mind and heart … to you I have entrusted my cause!

There is no more powerful and certain and expeditious way to have our problems solved than to "entrust our cause" to Jesus. We know this in theory, but in practice, the moment those trials come, we are tempted to stress, to worry, to puzzle over them; to lose sleep, to lose hope, to get angry, to despair. It is a *losing* battle to ruminate over problems that are not in our power to solve. Furthermore, such behavior will cause "a division [to] occur in the crowd."

The Pharisees in today's Gospel ruminated so much over how to solve their problem (that is, get rid of Jesus) that their imaginations led them to faulty assumptions and false conclusions. They used the "evidence" they believed to forcibly impose their argument (*The Christ will not come from Galilee, will he? Does not Scripture say that the Christ will be of David's family and come from Bethlehem?*). They were so rigid in their determination, that they had no room for any other possibility of thought, and their stubborn pride blinded them to the fact that the very Scripture passage they pointed to provided evidence *for* Jesus's divinity, not against it. Scripture *always* reveals truth.

Next, the guards try to open the eyes of the Pharisees by going around their argument, rather than try to take it head on:

Never before has anyone spoken like this man.

In other words, they were saying, "I don't understand why he's from Galilee, but I do know my heart has never burned before like this in my whole life. And it's not burning with anger or anxiety or distress. I have never been so full of peace and joy and love a single moment of my life."

But the Pharisees are still stuck on the Galilee point (*Have you also been deceived? … But this crowd, which does not know the law, is accursed … Look and see that no prophet arises from Galilee).* They do not think for a moment that they don't have their facts straight (nor do they care to know if they do); they are going to hold fast to the false information they have at all costs, simply because it "proves" what they want to believe. The Gospel passage ends here in division:

Then each went to his own house.

So how would the story have ended differently if instead of ruminating on their problems, riling up anger, anxiety, false assumptions, and their imaginations, the Pharisees had instead turned to God and prayed, "I don't like what's going on here. I don't trust this guy from Galilee, I think he's deceiving the crowd, and this is going to makes us all 'accursed.' But God, I know you're the one who allowed him to enter our lives. Please show us for what purpose. What would you have us do in this circumstance? We surrender this to you; please take care of this situation which threatens to destroy our faith."

Of course, the scenario would have ended *very* differently. The Pharisees would certainly have expected "the malice of the wicked come to an end," but the surprise would have been that *their* malice would have ended, not the "malice" of Jesus which existed only in their imaginations. Their surrender would have begotten them the same burning flame of peace and joy and love that the guards received in Jesus's presence, and they would have known in an instant exactly who this Jesus was. And in that moment, on their knees before the smiling face of Jesus, Jesus would have bent down and whispered in their ears, "By the way … I wasn't born in Galilee. I *am* from Bethlehem."

Surrender and trust is the antidote to *all* our difficulties, and the sooner we learn that, the sooner we will have the peace that surpasses all understanding. We will either receive the answer to our prayers exactly as we had hoped, or we will receive the gift of total detachment from the outcome, so that "what happens next" no longer has such a strong hold on our lives anymore. Either way, it's perfect. Just for today, the moment temptation to ruminate comes up (as it surely will), let us strive not to *think* so much — at least not before we have first prayed, "Jesus, I surrender this to You; You take care of it." Then let us witness the power of that prayer!

SOLEMNITY OF THE ANNUNCIATION OF THE LORD

(IS 7:10-14; 8:10; PS 40:7-11; HEB 10:4-10; LK 1:26-38)

But she was greatly troubled at what was said and pondered what sort of greeting this might be.

For all that Mary was "troubled" at the angel Gabriel's greeting, there is something so gentle and peaceful about this Annunciation scene. Certainly, the angel must have been terrible and mighty to behold, a sight that would have caused any of us to quake in our knees. But Mary, whose heart must surely have been pounding at the appearance of this divine apparition, restores her composure just as quickly as the presence of the angel would have alarmed her. How is this possible? Because Mary *ponders*. She takes the time to reflect before she reacts. Now, in the physical life, when one is trying to solve a puzzle, to better understand a befuddling circumstance, or to figure out the answer to a complicated problem, the act of pondering can take some time. But in the spiritual life, God can shed his insights upon mysterious situations the moment we ask. That is, he shows us his hand in our circumstances, though not necessarily does he reveal to us how the story ends. Such was the case with Mary's visit from the angel. Mary ponders, and the response she receives to her prayer — that the Holy Spirit would come upon her, and what's more, that her "barren" cousin of "old age" is well into her second trimester of pregnancy — is enough for Mary's peace to be restored. She may have found the idea of being virgin mother to the Messiah daunting (to say the least), but she is completely at peace with it, because although she could not possibly foresee all that her assigned mission would entail in the future, she could see God's hand in her circumstance *now*. And as long as God had this, she would be good with whatever he had planned.

We could learn a lot from Mary (obviously). But on this solemnity of the Annunciation, Mary teaches us specifically to "consider the word of God," and to try "to understand it in its entirety" (Pope Benedict XVI, *Jesus of Nazareth: The Infancy Narratives*). When troubling and disconcerting events come our way, let us resist the temptation to jump to conclusions, to breathe into a paper bag as we are overwhelmed by anxiety, or to grab a pitchfork and protest circumstances we immediately assume are "unfair." Let's instead imitate Mary, who, in the words of Pope Benedict XVI, "seeks to understand the context, the overall significance of God's message." What is God doing in this confusing and befuddling circumstance? Perhaps we don't understand it — perhaps it's not ours to understand right now — but can we at least ask God to reveal what *he* is doing in all this? After all, God is *never* out of the picture when it comes to our trials, so we must stop acting as though he were, every time something stressful pops up. Trusting God does not translate into "doing nothing." Trusting God merely gives us the grace to remain peaceful, so that we are then in a disposition to be attentive to whatever God may (or may not) ask us to do. So the next time we are "greatly troubled," like Mary, let's not panic.

A simple "thank you" will do.

FIFTH SUNDAY OF LENT

EZ 37:12-14; PS 130:1-8; ROM 8:8-11; JN 11:1-45 (YEAR A)
JER 31:31-34; PS 51: 2-4, 12-15; HEB 5: 7-9; JN 12: 20-33 (YEAR B)
IS 43: 16-21; PS 126: 1-6; PHIL 3: 8-14; JN 8:1-11 (YEAR C)

Now it springs forth, do you not perceive it?

It is human nature to hold on to cherished memories. As a friend once pointed out to me, often we keep those memories close to our hearts through little "mementos" that remind us of past events. A vacation photo, for example, will be framed and placed on the mantle, calling to mind for us the wonderful time spent at the ocean with family. Every time we dust that frame, a warmth fills our hearts as we recall the fond remembrance of that precious occasion. But some of the "mementos" we hold on to are not so pleasant, are they? Maybe we have some photos that remind us of an awful time in our lives. They bring us right back to the resentment and anxiety we felt in the past. What was that?? We thought we had forgiven the offense long ago! The thing is, forgiveness is not always a one-time event. It is usually more of a process, one whose resolution needs to be renewed time and again. It begins with the *desire* to forgive — which is enough for the Lord. Our goodwill, and not our feelings, is the measure God uses to determine whether have made the effort to forgive our neighbor. But desire is only a start. In order for our forgiveness to be *complete*, we must "forget."

Remember not the events of the past, the things of long ago consider not; see,

I am doing something new!

To forget, in this sense, does not mean to erase memories we are not capable of erasing; it means to *let go* of the mementos we've been holding on to for a "rainy day." "Proof" that we were unjustly wounded, that we were on the side of right and the offender on the side of wrong, lest it should escape our memory. A friend once told me when I was having trouble forgiving someone, "Forgiveness is not about rehashing the past. It's about: where do we go from here?"

… *forgetting what lies behind but straining forward to what lies ahead* …

So we measure our forgiveness by our desire … But how do we make ourselves "let go" in order that our forgiveness may be *complete*? So often when we think of times in the past when we truly let go of unforgiveness, it seems that it just … kind of happened. It's not that we don't remember that the hurtful event took place, but now we're fuzzy on the details, we couldn't retell the story clearly because we're not even sure anymore who started what; in fact, the only thing that stands out in our minds is all the ways in which we ourselves contributed to the problem! This is the sign to us that the Holy Spirit is working in us and through us to make us "forget" the past. When God directs us to forget, what he really means is: "Stop pointing at your neighbor's speck and work on your own log before you trip over it!" So if we want to forget the past, if we want to truly let go of old resentments, we have to start by asking the Holy Spirit just one question: "What have I done to contribute to *their* wound?"

Yikes. Who wants to hear the answer to that question? I know I don't … and yet if it will give me sweet relief from the oppressive grip that unforgiveness has on me … then I do. It is going to be a painful, awful place to go, but also a sweet place because we'll be there with Jesus. He does ask us to look at our misery … and it is *awful*. But he does not ask us to look there without looking at him too. And those eyes of love and tenderness and compassion offer us the most overwhelming sweetness we could possibly experience. No consolation could be greater than the consolation of his mercy.

In the desert I make a way … for I put water in the desert and rivers in the wasteland for my chosen people to drink …

The reason it is so hard for us to let go is that we must go into the desert first. A "wasteland" in which we view the thorny filth of our sinfulness.

For I do not do what I want, but I do what I hate. (Rom 7:19)

That desert experience does not generally last for just a moment either; it may last four days, forty days, or even forty years. But that's ok, because even though it's hard, it's painful, it's burning, Jesus will always give us the water of consolation we need along the way … if we give *up* our distractions and give *him* our trust. It is our perseverance that will yield a harvest.

It is not that I have already taken hold of it or have already attained perfect maturity, but I continue my pursuit in hope that I may possess it, since I have indeed been taken possession of by Christ Jesus.

MONDAY OF THE FIFTH WEEK OF LENT

(DN 13:1-9, 15-17, 19-30, 33-62; PS 23:1-6; JN 8:1-11)

They said this to test him, so that they could have some charge to bring against him. Jesus bent down and began to write on the ground with his finger.

Boy, would I love to have been a fly on the wall in this scene. One can just picture the loud voices, the heated tempers, the aggressive pushing and shoving of this adulterous woman by her accusers, ready to pick a fight with Jesus and inflict violent punishment upon their "sinner" in custody. And Jesus? He remains cool as a cucumber. It is amazing. Because what is the normal human reaction when someone is accusing, testing, or otherwise inciting us to argue? We argue back. We take the bait. No, we don't want to. And we certainly regret reacting this way when someone's temper has flared up in our presence. But it is almost involuntary ... you yawn, I yawn; you laugh, I laugh. And in the case of someone throwing accusations around ... you attack, I attack, or at least get defensive.

Not so with Jesus. His plan of "attack" in defense of the woman is ... to remain silent. His very first response is to say absolutely nothing. But although Jesus says nothing, he *does* something rather curious: he begins to "write on the ground with his finger." The Scribes and Pharisees must have thought they had finally trapped him: Jesus was at a loss for words — *Ha*! So, as anyone who would take another's silence as a sign of agreement, they press him further. (*Huh? Huh? What do you have to say for yourself now? Still think you're above the law of Moses?*)

Then, in a dramatic pause, Jesus "straightens up." One can imagine him cease his writing, first looking at the words he has written, the words nobody bothered to read. Then, shifting his glance from his words to look straight into the eyes of the accusers, and with a penetrating glance that sees into their souls, Jesus finally speaks:

Let the one among you who is without sin be the first to throw a stone ...

Was it his spoken words that finally convinced the Pharisees and Scribes to back down? Perhaps. And yet, it is hard to imagine that these men, full of pride, would ever admit — even to themselves — to being "with" sin. When all one looks at is the wrongdoing of others, one becomes blind to one's own.

One of my pet peeves is finding "stuff" on the counter, especially if it is a counter I have just taken an hour to clear off and organize. That is ... I am annoyed *only* if the stuff that's on the counter was placed there by *other* people. If it is *my* stuff, somehow, I don't notice it. Such would have been the experience of the Pharisees with regard to their own wrongdoings. Like the elders in today's first reading, they would have "suppressed their consciences" when it came to their own sins but would have held up a magnifying glass when it came to examining the sins of others. So it's hard to imagine Jesus's spoken words would have had much of an effect on their thinking.

Again he bent down and wrote on the ground.

But what about his written word? One imagines that after Jesus spoke, then calmly resumed his writing, this time the Pharisees would have turned their gaze from Jesus to the ground. They would have wondered, perhaps exasperated: *What could he be writing that is more important than discussing the accusation we've just presented to him?*

Scripture does not reveal the answer to that question, but theologians have offered some possibilities. One such possibility is that Jesus was writing down the sins of the very Pharisees and Scribes who were doing the accusing. Can we imagine this? A list, as it were, that would not have named names but would have been easily recognizable to the one reading it. We can imagine:

1. *Slept with his brother's wife*
2. *Stole from his deceased brother's widow*
3. *Disavowed his illegitimate child*
4. *Met secretly with his mistress*

And on and on. We can envision that when each of the accusers recognized his own sin — written right there on the ground, exposed for everyone to see — *that* would have been the one thing that would have struck them speechless. Without raising his voice, without arguing, debating, getting defensive or getting violent, Jesus has silenced them. His only weapon was *Fear of the Lord.* The Pharisees and Scribes would have experienced fear in that moment — such that they had never known before. They would have been terrified of being exposed, terrified that others would find out what they had worked so diligently to keep hidden in the dark. And the ones who would have been most terrified of exposure would have been the ones who were the greatest offenders: the elders. These were the greatest offenders, not because of the degree of their offense, but because they held the highest office and therefore should have been setting the most virtuous example:

And in response, they went away one by one, BEGINNING with the elders.

As we find out later, though Jesus's words did indeed instill fear in these men, it was a fear that was misplaced. When the words of Jesus cause us to tremble, they are meant to inspire us to greater reverence and awe of the Almighty, which then should lead us to greater love of God and gratitude for his incredible mercy upon us, a mercy we do not deserve. It is this awareness of his unconditional love and gratitude for his unfathomable mercy that inspires us to "go and sin no more." But this is not how the Scribes and Pharisees receive Jesus's words. They receive his words as a counterattack, and therefore would go on later to try to stone him (Jn 10:31) and arrest him (Jn 10:39). It is incredible to think they still could not bring themselves to draw the conclusion that Jesus indeed is the Son of God. How else did they imagine he knew so much about them? Temple gossip? Whatever it was Jesus wrote on the ground, his words, "Let the one among you who is without sin be the first to throw a stone at her" would have said to them in no uncertain terms that Jesus was calling each of them "sinner." To a truly righteous one, this would have incited normal human defensiveness; but instead, these men had no defense. To be blind at this point to who Jesus was would have been willful ignorance. The Pharisees and Scribes simply did not want to see.

Then Jesus straightened up and said to her, "Woman, where are they? Has no one condemned you?"

Once again, Jesus "straightens up." Just like he had done moments before with the accusers, Jesus looks straight into the eyes of the woman, and offers a penetrating glance into her soul. It is a look that says, "I know you." But do you know what? It is a look that would have been accompanied by the warmest and most loving smile she had ever known. It would have been a smile that would have wiped away all her human fear, and immediately restored peace to her soul. This woman, in her deepest shame, who, unlike Susanna, was truly guilty of the crimes she was accused of, and who, according to the law of Moses, *deserved* the punishment of stoning ... has now been *loved* by the Teacher, in a way she had never known before. It is a love that is accompanied by untold mercy, one that says, "I love you exactly as you are."

Neither do I condemn you.

And then, our Gospel passage ends with the most powerful and inspiring words Jesus could ever say to any one of us:

Go, and from now on do not sin any more.

This woman's life was turned around not by fear, not by threats, not by punishment, but by one force alone: unconditional love and mercy. *Love* is the most powerful tool the Father has given us at our disposal to turn the hearts of lost souls back to him. So let's love these souls as Jesus does: unconditionally, mercifully, without raising our voices and without losing our peace. We indeed must be instruments of his message: "Go and sin no more." But if we want others to heed these words, then we have no greater weapon of "attack" in the battle for their souls than to offer them Christ's merciful and unconditional love.

> *Even though I walk in the dark valley I fear no evil, for you are at my side.*

TUESDAY OF THE FIFTH WEEK OF LENT

(NUM 21:4-9; PS 102: 2-3, 16-21; JN 8:21-30)

But with their patience worn out by the journey, the people complained against God ...

The approach of Easter break is the time of year when my kids begin to "check out" when it comes to school. The days start to get longer, the sun shines brighter and warmer, and the birds begin chirping once again, signaling the promise of summer. Everybody is just *done* with homework, including this homeschooling mom, whose patience, like that of the ancient Israelites, has been "worn out by the journey." This time of year, half of my day is spent wrangling kids back to attention, spewing empty threats, and otherwise feeling exasperated. Any mother can understand the complaining and self-pity of one who is having a hard day, even though the day itself is a gift. So why is God so hard on these Israelites, so severe in the discipline he has meted out upon them?

In punishment the LORD sent among the people seraph serpents, which bit the people so that many of them died.

Yeesh, the punishment hardly seems to fit the crime! After all, we understand that complaining begets ingratitude and only makes a miserable person all the more miserable ... but these people *did* endure 400 years of slavery. Was it not understandable that the children of Israel should have some trust issues? The thing is ...

God did not punish the Israelites for having trouble remaining cheerful when they were having a "hard day." The Father, who is "kind and merciful, slow to anger, and rich in compassion" (Ps 145:8), takes pity on us when we are struggling. But let's compare this passage to a similar one that occurs later:

> *Here in the wilderness the whole Israelite community grumbled against Moses and Aaron. The Israelites said to them, "If only we had died at the LORD's hand in the land of Egypt, as we sat by our kettles of meat and ate our fill of bread! But you have led us into this wilderness to make this whole assembly die of famine!" Then the LORD said to Moses: I am going to rain down bread from heaven for you. Each day the people are to go out and gather their daily portion; thus will I test them, to see whether they follow my instructions or not…* (Ex 16:2-4)

So why does the Lord this time give the Israelites food to eat in response to their "grumbling," when he had delivered a terrifying punishment in response to their "complaining" before? Let's compare the two scenes. In the first instance, on their journey, the people complained:

> *Why have you brought us up from Egypt to die in this desert, where there is no food or water?*

Legitimate complaint, right? Who doesn't get grouchy when one is hungry? The thing is ... the people *weren't* hungry. How do we know this? Because of what they say next:

> *We are disgusted with this wretched food!*

So was there "no food," or was there indeed food? Which was it?

Sometimes when my kids rummage through our pantry — which is filled to the brim with bread, peanut butter, cereal, and canned goods — and then shift to examine the contents of the refrigerator, inspecting the eggs, the milk, the bread, and the lunch meat ... after all their extensive investigation, they will determine, with sourpuss faces, that there is "nothing" to eat. What they really mean to say is that we're out of cookies, potato chips, and ice cream. When they whine that they are "starving," I remind them that there are children in the world who are *actually* going without food right now, so they can have a better understanding of what that word means. Such was the disposition of the children of Israel on their journey. Their idea of "no food" was simply that they were missing the steak and potatoes of the old days. But they were not *literally* starving. In fact, if they were hungry at all, it was by their own choice, snubbing their noses at the food that was available to them, simply because they were tired of it. Now let's remember the Lord is "*rich* in compassion." What does that mean? It means that he takes pity on us when we are having a hard time with eating the same food over and over again. He will even do something about it — *if* our hands are raised in *gratitude*, and not complaint. Recently a friend with a muscular disability told me she has the physical ability to cook, but it is the same two foods over and over, because that is what her body allows her to accomplish. But she then added: "By the grace of God, I don't get tired of either!"

In her gratitude, God found a way to multiply my friend's two "cents"— all she has to offer — into something both nourishing and satisfying for her. That is what gratitude does: it begets grace. One wonders what God's mercy would have done for the Israelites if only they had not stopped at lamenting about their suffering, but instead ended with, "Thank you for feeding us." Perhaps the Lord would have turned the food they were sick of eating into an enjoyable meal, surrounded by the joy of their family and friends.

So let's compare this scene to the one that comes later, in which the Israelites grumble again. This time, in the wilderness, the people truly have no food. They *really* are about to "die of famine." They still shamefully lack trust in God, despite everything he has done for them, but this time, they really have been pushed to their limits. So God's plan is to take care of their needs, by "raining down bread from heaven," but it would be delivered in such a way as to *test* them: they were only to take their daily portion, and not hoard any, even though it went against their every instinct, having just endured the terrible hunger that famine causes. The Lord understood their complaint and would offer them the chance to prove that it was out of weakness, and not because their hearts had turned against him. This would be their opportunity to trust that the Father would take care of their needs.

So what do we learn today? First, today's passage from Exodus teaches us that when our patience is "worn out," it is then we must redouble our efforts to give God praise and thanks. The alternative is to allow our difficulty to fester into complaints about things that are not even true. Recently, when my own patience was worn out, I went from recognizing that Mondays are a challenge for anybody, let alone a six-year-old, to complaining that my child "never" listens. Mercifully, a good old-fashioned examen prayer enabled me to catch myself before I threw myself headlong down a rabbit-hole, and I remembered to turn to God for help. Immediately, my load was lightened (or at least it seemed so to me; in the words of my friend, by the grace of God, I did not "get tired" of homeschooling!), and my mood lifted. Peace was once again restored to my soul, and I was able to return to my duties with a smile on my face and joy in my heart. That is what praise and thanks will do.

> "Cheerfulness strengthens the heart and makes us persevere in a good life. Therefore the servant of God ought always to be in good spirits." –St. Philip Neri

The second lesson we learn from the lament of the Israelites is about *trust*. Specifically, that Jesus will take care of our *daily* needs, even if we do not know how the story ends, and even though the temptation to take matters into our own hands is very great. Sometimes it can feel to us like God has led us into the desert for "nothing." We thought his journey was going to take us from Y to Z, and instead we find ourselves back at X, worse off than before we even started! *Why did you lead us out to the desert, Lord, only to make things worse? It was supposed to be better — isn't that what You promised? We were better off before, having no hope in a promise that wasn't to come true!*

Friends, on the days we feel like this, it is then we must look at the "bronze pole" hanging right up on our wall. The Cross of Christ will show us just how much God will keep his promise, how much he loves us, and how much we can trust him. Jesus never leaves us, never forgets his promise … *even* when things seem to have gone from bad to worse. It is then we must exclaim all the more, "Jesus, I trust in You!" And with this simple act of humble gratitude, Jesus *will* change the circumstances or change our hearts.

The one who sent me is with me. He has not left me alone…

WEDNESDAY OF THE FIFTH WEEK OF LENT

(DN 3:14-20, 52-56, 91-92, 95; JN 8:31-42)

Jesus said to those Jews who believed in him, "If you remain in my word, you will truly be my disciples, and you will know the truth, and the truth will set you free."

There seems to be a strange irony here in today's passage from John (actually, there are a few strange ironies — but for the sake of brevity, we will examine just one). Jesus today shifts his attention from the Jews and Pharisees who remain in their stubborn pride, to the "many [who] came to believe in him [because] he spoke this way" (Jn 8:30). He tells them if they "remain" in his word, the one they have come to believe, they will be set free. How glorious! But then a strange thing happens. Just a few verses later, Jesus tells these very people, the ones who "believed" in him:

... you are trying to kill me, because my word has no room among you ... You are doing the works of your father!

In other words, Jesus is now calling the very people who were listening to him, spawn of the devil! What on earth is going on here?

Scripture scholars have noted several inconsistencies in this passage, attributing them to the "many non-Johannine features in the language," and the "many doubtful readings within the passage" (bible.usccb.org). According to these scholars, it is likely certain verses were not penned by John at all, but rather, were later inserted into the text to fit an allusion to the prophetic accounts of earlier Scriptures. Regardless, what "[has been] written [has been] written" (Jn 19:22), and as part of sacred Scripture, we cannot simply chalk up an inconsistency to something that did not *actually* happen that way, giving it no more than a cursory glance. Rather, the fact that this passage remains — *as is* — suggests there is something the Holy Spirit wants us to learn from these precise words, something that has to do with a *spiritual* lesson, and not simply a historical one, the same way all Scripture is meant to be read. So what can we learn from this seeming inconsistency — that the ones Jesus addresses who came to believe, are the very same ones trying to kill him?

> *They answered him, "We are descendants of Abraham and have never been enslaved to anyone. How can you say, 'You will become free'?"*

The answer, perhaps, lies in the response of those who have come to believe. When Jesus tells them that if they "remain" in his word they will be set free, it is at this moment, it would seem, that "Satan entered" them, just as he did Judas (Lk 22:3). They went from believing to disbelieving — in literally that single instant. It happened that fast. In other words, Jesus began by speaking to the Jews (and quite likely the Pharisees) who came to believe ... but by the time he was done speaking, these same men were back to being part of the mob who "picked up stones to throw at him" (Jn 8:59). What happened that changed their minds so quickly?

> *We are descendants of Abraham and have never been enslaved to anyone.*

This group of Jews has just had their *pride* stirred up by the Lord. When I was a teenager, I had a personal experience, which I told few people about. But someone heard about it and started asking me a lot of probing questions. They were harmless questions, but they were ones I did not want to answer, simply because it was an experience I was not prepared to share. But they would not let it go, and I felt that I was backed into a corner. My response was to overreact to the whole thing. The thing is, all these years later, when that subject comes up, interiorly I still overreact all over again! For me, it is a personal trigger that stirs up my defenses. And for the Jews of first century Jerusalem, their trigger was the word, "slavery."

Now of course, Jesus did not even use the word "slavery" initially; all he said was that the Jews would be set "free." But the implication was enough to get them on the defensive:

We are descendants of Abraham and have never been enslaved to anyone.

Um … yes, they have. Try four hundred years of it! The blatant denial of their ancestral enslavement was a result of their overreaction to a truth that was evidently still very, very painful for the people of Israel. In their minds, the promise of a Messiah had still not come, even after centuries of faithfulness. It would seem Jesus's words to them are a stark reminder of that, resurfacing all the anger they had felt at a perceived injustice by God of his unfulfilled promise. And what hope they'd had that Jesus could be the Savior that had finally come, was apparently crushed the moment they were reminded of where they had been. All the resentment they had suppressed over their ancestral history — the humiliation of their people, the *chosen* ones, who had been held in captivity for so long — came bubbling up to the surface, exploding in animosity toward the Savior.

It is no coincidence that Jesus's first words of admonition to the Jews who came to believe in him were: "remain in my word." Jesus knows just how easily the faith that one has worked so hard to possess can be lost, and it is an admonition we would do well to heed ourselves today. Friends, when trials, sufferings, or "triggers" that remind us of our past wounds come up, they threaten to veer us off the path we "have come to believe" to be true. *Every time.*

What if this doesn't end well this time? What if our faith doesn't really work that way? I want to be loving — but this person makes it so hard!

It is only by *remaining* in his word that we will overcome the temptations that assault us. But let's make no mistake: Jesus never said we will be free of those temptations. In fact, as we advance in the spiritual life, very often God will allow the heat to turn up a notch, in order to encourage us to *grow*. No, Jesus does not promise us freedom from temptation, but rather, freedom from *sin*. What does that mean? It means that the more we remain in his word (by seeking refuge in Scripture, prayer, and the Sacraments the moment those temptations come), the less those temptations will be temptations for us … until one day, they will cease to disturb us, no matter how fast and furious they come. Can we even imagine that kind of freedom? It truly is the most glorious life imaginable! So for today, let's practice what it means to remain in Jesus's word. When the temptation to complain, to get angry, to doubt, or to worry comes up — and it surely will — let's look away from the temptation, if only for a moment, and with what little strength we have, turn instead to our Jesus. A simple, "Jesus, I trust in You," is all it takes to begin to have our clarity and peace once again restored.

> *Blessed are they who have kept the word with a generous heart and yield a harvest through perseverance …* (Lk 8:15)

THURSDAY OF THE FIFTH WEEK OF LENT

(GN 17:3-9; PS 105:4-9; JN 8:51-59)

And if I should say that I do not know him, I would be like you a liar.

Wow. Yesterday we heard Jesus declare to the Jews that they are "doing the works of [their] father" — that is, Satan; and today we hear Jesus denounce them as liars. The Lord sure does not mince words, does he? If he had any interest at all in keeping the few disciples who had come to believe in him, to encourage them in their newly forming faith, he certainly does not appear to be trying.

Years ago, I had a friend who had suffered through a traumatic experience in her life — one that shook her to the core — and she began to ponder deeply the meaning of life. For her, the search began with the Church. She turned to me with lots of questions; we would spend long hours deep into the night discussing the things of faith over the phone. I made myself available to her whenever she needed to talk, because my heart just broke for her. I wanted to do everything I could to encourage her in her faith journey, eager to help her come to know the love and mercy of Christ.

Such was not the way Our Lord appears to treat his newfound followers in today's Gospel. He is not gentle or encouraging, understanding how difficult it must have been for them to accept this radical preacher whose ways were just so … *different.* Instead,

Jesus *insults* them. But whatever for? Well, we know for certain it could not have been to drive them away. So what could have been his motive? Let's recall that the Lord commands us to love him "with *all* [our] heart, with *all* [our] soul, and with *all* [our] mind" (Mt 22:37). That means that our faith does not collapse or waver when "the rain [falls], the floods [come], and the winds [blow] and [buffet] the house" (Mt 7:25). Jesus was not "insulting" the Jews in an attempt to pick a fight with them, pit himself against them, or discourage them in their faith. He was calling them out for what lay deep down in the hidden recesses of their hearts, in order to *root it out.*

My husband is very organized and logical, and believes if you're going to do a job, you do it right. It is a work ethic he inherited from his father, the upside of which is that when my husband takes on a project, it is done to perfection. The downside … is that we have to wait for the results, because he's not going to do a half-hearted job. Me? After decades of identifying with "the little old lady who lived in a shoe," I have "perfected" the art of multitasking. Which is code for: lots of things get done; few get done well. For example, I can cook a delicious meal, but the table setting usually has cups or napkins missing. I can keep up with the laundry, but my idea of ironing is to give the clothes a good shake when they come out of the dryer. It is simply how I have learned to manage the endless list of household chores I have to do with the large-sized family I have. My husband and I are quite compatible housemates, but suffice it to say, "his ways are not my ways." So when my husband offers me a "suggestion," my initial reaction is to feel defensive. I think to myself, *Easy for him to say when he gets to go to work and is not the one doing these chores!* But then, after I take a moment to chew on his words, I must admit … my husband is usually right. And even on the days I don't see things the same way that he does, not once can I say that my husband has ever suggested anything with the intention of insulting me, belittling me, or hurting my feelings. Always, always, his intention is love. He just wants things to be better — not for himself — but for *me.*

When Jesus called the Jews out for "doing the works of [their] father" and for being "liars," his intention was not to hurt their feelings. Rather, just as was his intention when he said to Peter,

"Get behind me Satan!" (Mt 16:23), Jesus's intention now is to *rectify* their motives. He was pointing out what they had previously been blind to, so they could *change* that which they could now see! That they chose to stone him instead is not an indication of Jesus's "error" in speaking out boldly as he did to the Jews; rather, it is an indication of their own hardness of heart. Once the truth of Jesus's words "rained" down on them, sadly, their faith in him "collapsed and was completely ruined" (Mt 7:27). In the end, the "believing" that they had begun to come to was indeed sincere, but it had been built on a foundation of "sand."

If today you hear his voice, harden not your hearts. (Ps 95:8)

FRIDAY OF THE FIFTH WEEK OF LENT

(JER 20:10-13; PS 18:2-7; JN 10:31-42)

I hear the whisperings of many ... those who were my friends are on the watch for any misstep of mine.

Anyone who has experienced the heartache of betrayal can identify with the utter pain and anguish at the sound of Jeremiah's words. Someone who you thought you could trust, who you thought was a *friend* ... proved not to be the person you thought they were. There is hardly any experience that is more disconcerting: it makes one question one's judgment, it leaves one afraid to trust again. If such has been the case for us, to a greater or lesser degree, let us take heart. Never do we resemble Our Lord more than when we have been betrayed and abandoned by someone we once called "friend."

But the LORD is with me ... my persecutors will stumble, they will not triumph. In their failure they will be put to ... confusion.

So is Jeremiah's story a lesson in the vengeance the Lord will take upon those who persecute us so that, in the end, we get the last laugh? Old Testament Scripture can sometimes have a tone of revenge to it ... but this is not the kind of "triumph" God obtains for those who turn to him for help. The kind of triumph the Father offers us is not over other people, but over *ourselves*:

O LORD of hosts, you who test the just, who probe mind and hear ... to you I have entrusted my cause.

St. Catherine of Siena tells us that, according to Jesus, it is the *Father* who permits the trials that tempt us to fear, to distrust, to anger, to unforgiveness ... *so that* we learn to grow:

> "I've appointed the Devil to tempt and to trouble My creatures in this life … not so that My creatures will be overcome, but so that they may overcome, proving their virtue … Neither the Devil nor any other creature can control [your] free will … if you don't consent to his temptations and harassments — you will never be injured by the guilt of sin in any temptation. Instead, you'll actually be strengthened by the temptation ..."

The triumph over our enemies that the Lord offers us is not vengeance upon the ones who have caused our pain, but rather, triumph over the temptations that threaten to take away our peace.

Sing to the LORD, praise the LORD …

When we turn to the Lord with a song of gratitude upon our lips, he replaces the disturbance in our souls with peace in our hearts:

Praised be the LORD, I exclaim, and I am safe from my enemies.

In today's Gospel, no one has been betrayed by those once called friends more than Jesus. Even the sound of Jesus's voice is like a shock wave to their every last nerve, and the people have had enough:

Then they tried again to arrest him; but he escaped from their power.

Actually, they have "had enough" *before:*

So they tried to arrest him, but no one laid a hand upon him, because his hour had not yet come. (Jn 7:30)

And *before:*

So they picked up stones to throw at him; but Jesus hid and went out of the temple area… (Jn 8:59)

And *before*:

[They] led him to the brow of the hill on which their town had been built, to hurl him down headlong. But he passed through the midst of them and went away. (Lk 4:29-30)

These had to be chaotic, mystifying scenes. What must have been going through the minds of the people who “tried” to arrest and kill Jesus, but could not? They didn’t believe he was the Son of God, so what other hypothesis did they have to explain how he kept vanishing from their grip?

Have [they] no fear of God? (Lk 23:40)

Evidently ones such as these had no fear of God. At least not in terms of Fear of the Lord as a gift of the Holy Spirit. Fear of the Lord is the gift that enables a soul to see the hand of divine providence in one’s circumstances. Without it, one is spiritually blind. Now before we go thanking God that we are not like those blind Jews, let's understand that this gift is pretty fluid. If we don't "use it, we lose it," just like with speaking the foreign language we learned in high school. So how do we speak the language of Fear of the Lord? By praising and thanking God in all things. And let's remember, just like with French or Spanish, it's a *foreign* language — meaning, it's not going to come naturally to us to thank God in adversity. At least not without *practice*. And lots of it — daily and continually. That is why it is so easy to lose the gift of Fear of the Lord, and it's also why it's a gift so few possess. We have to work really hard to place ourselves in a disposition to receive this grace. After all, who wants to thank God for the friend who has betrayed him? Nobody does. But, like Jeremiah, let’s do it anyway. In this way, the Lord will "rescue the life of the poor from the power of the wicked!"

One last note. Turning to Jesus in praise and thanks when we have been betrayed does not mean that betrayal isn't going to hurt. Jesus had a heart bursting with gratitude continually, one that was totally at peace ... but he also felt the pain of rejection deeply. Very deeply. When he escaped from those who were trying to arrest him, he was not just attempting to avoid prison. We already have seen that Jesus does not have to ever run away in order to do that; if it's not his time, one *word* from his sacred lips is all it takes to stop his persecutors in their tracks. He was not actually escaping *from* anyone or anything. He was escaping *to* something else. But to what?

> *He went back across the Jordan to the place where John first baptized, and there he remained.*

In one of his darkest moments, why is it that the Lord goes back to the place of his baptism? Because it is here that he finds the solace and comfort of the friends who truly love him, who truly stand by him, who believe in him, and who follow him:

> *After all the people had been baptized and Jesus also had been baptized and was praying, heaven was opened and the holy Spirit descended upon him in bodily form like a dove. And a voice came from heaven, "You are my beloved Son; with you I am well pleased."* (Lk 3:21-22)

In that single moment of Christ's baptism, there was no denying that Jesus was indeed the Messiah. It is true, these could have been a people, who, like the Jews across the Jordan, did not possess the gift of Fear of the Lord and therefore in their blindness, could have explained away the supernatural event involving the dove and the divine voice as their eyes and ears deceiving them, a total coincidence, or even "just" a dream. But evidently, they did indeed possess that gift. These were a people who had prepared themselves to receive it, after a lifetime of singing hymns of gratitude to God in all their circumstances. And on that day of their baptism, they received the "eyes to see and ears to hear" (Mt 13:16).

> *And many there began to believe in him.*

SATURDAY OF THE FIFTH WEEK OF LENT

(EZ 37:21-28; JER 31:10-13; JN 11:45-56)

Many of the Jews who had come to Mary and seen what Jesus had done began to believe in him. But some of them went to the Pharisees and told them what Jesus had done.

Who are these "some" that went to the Pharisees to tell them about Jesus? Were they among the Jews who had come to Mary but did not believe, as opposed to the "many" others who did? Not likely. Let's recall that the reason these "many" came to believe in Jesus is that the ones who "had come to Mary" were there to comfort her in her mourning over the death of her brother Lazarus. In fact, they were grieving too:

... the Jews ... had come with her weeping... (Jn 11:33)

So their coming to believe was not due to passing fancy, emotion, or opinion; it was based on *fact.* They had witnessed for themselves the impossible: a man dead for four days, raised to life from the tomb. There was no other explanation but that the supernatural was at play here.

Thus, the "some" who went to the Pharisees were indeed believers. Why, then, go to the Pharisees at all, knowing that so many of them were plotting against the Savior? Scripture does not reveal the answer to that question. It seems, as Mary's friends, it would be unlikely they were "snitching." At the very least, they would have needed some time to process the magnitude of what had just transpired. What seems more likely is that in their great exuberance over having their friend back, and at having witnessed the incredible miracle that proved to them that the Messiah had finally come, these "some" ran excitedly to those in ecclesiastical authority to announce to them the *Good News*! Their motive, it would seem, was to win the Pharisees over, that they might partake in the Savior's love and mercy too.

How ever it was they came — perhaps boldly rejoicing — and whatever it was they said — perhaps speaking excitedly all at once — it was a *convincing* argument. How do we know this? Because of what the chief priests said next:

This man is performing many signs.

In other words, the chief priests and the Pharisees did not leave their conversation with these new believers unbelieving themselves; rather, they were convinced every word of what they said was true: Lazarus, who was dead, was now alive, thanks to the miracle Jesus had procured. Which makes what they say next so ... *odd*, to say the least:

If we leave him alone, all will believe in him, and the Romans will come and take away both our land and our nation.

"All will believe in him." They were afraid they would lose their authority over the people ... to *God*. Incredulously, the Pharisees did not want Jesus gone because they thought he was a fraud, or, as they had previously accused him, because they thought he was a "blasphemer." Rather, they now knew that what he was saying was true! Jesus indeed had just proved his divinity to them. So why were they still plotting against him? Perhaps because they simply did not *care*.

There was a blockbuster movie that came out in the early 90's called *The Fugitive*, starring Harrison Ford and Tommy Lee Jones. It was a remake of a popular series from decades before. The story is of a doctor, played by Harrison Ford, who is accused of a murder he did not commit. He is on the run, trying to prove his innocence. In one scene, after weeks of following the evidence of where this man has been, finding clue after clue that prove the man on the run is indeed innocent, the Marshall, played by Tommy Lee Jones, finally catches up with the fugitive. With his hands raised in surrender, the fugitive pleads with the Marshall, "I didn't do this." And the Marshall pauses, looks at him intently, and replies in an emphatic but unemotional tone: *I don't care.*

Like this Marshall, the Pharisees were so caught up with the job they had to do, that they forgot what it was even for, and they allowed no room for change or growth. When my husband and I first got married, we went out on a dinner date every Friday night. We thoroughly enjoyed it and decided it was important for us to keep the routine going. So when my first baby was born, we would simply plop him in his baby carrier and bring him along. Then my second was born — a challenge to bring two children to a restaurant, no doubt, but on the other hand, she was an easy baby, so it was manageable. Then I had twins. As unimaginable as it may seem, we kept our Friday night routine going. My husband and I were so caught up in keeping a routine we had once enjoyed, that we could not even see that what we were keeping now caused us nothing but stress. I am not sure how long it took us, but one night I looked at my husband across the table as I was bouncing one baby on my lap while feeding the other, and I said to him, "Are we enjoying this anymore?" He looked back at me in relief, shook his head, and that was the end of our Friday night ritual.

The Pharisees were so caught up in the trees, they could not see the forest. Jesus was so disturbing to them in their practice of the faith, they could not see that he *was* the faith! The prospect of losing the admiration and respect of the people, and their land and nation by the Romans, was of greater concern to them than losing the God who gave them their people, their land and their nation to begin with. It was the irony of ironies, that the very keepers of the faith, in their misguided effort to hold on to what they'd had, should be the ones who sought now to crush it.

Caiaphas, who was high priest that year, said to them, "You know

> *nothing, nor do you consider that it is better for you that one man should die instead of the people, so that the whole nation may not perish."*

More irony here. First, that Caiaphas should utter such prophetic words without realizing it ("he did not say this on his own"), and secondly, that he, who himself knew nothing of the prophecy he has just spoken, should say to the *others*, "you know nothing." But as is the way of the Lord, what Caiaphas intended for evil, God intended for good.

Early in my marriage, my second pregnancy ended in miscarriage. Coming home from the hospital the day I suffered such loss, my mother-in-law said to me, "One year from now you'll be holding a baby in your arms." Now, she was not pretending to be a self-proclaimed prophet; she was just trying to help me feel better in my time of sorrow. But the crazy thing is … it was one year later — to the *day* — that my next baby was born. My mother-in-law's words turned out to be prophetic, without her intending them to be.

Caiaphas too never intended to be part of the prophetic unfolding of salvation history, but unbeknownst to him, indeed he was. What he intended for personal glory, God intended for the glory of his Son. And today, Caiaphas has gone down in history in notoriety. This is what happens to anyone who stubbornly rejects grace.

Our lesson today then? Friends, let's notice the trees ... but only with the forest in mind. That is, let's remember our end goal: to reach heaven at the end of our earthly lives and to bring as many souls as we can with us. How can we possibly attain that goal if we spend our time nitpicking over *he said this* and *she said that*? It is not easy, to be sure. Because sometimes what "he said" is really hurtful, and sometimes what "she said" is really awful. How do we just let it go? By remembering that "Even though [they] meant harm to me, God meant it for good" (Gen 50:20). God is the author of all things, and if we have placed our lives in his beloved hands, then we have absolutely nothing over which to get our feathers ruffled. So let us be at peace. Jesus will take care of everything.

I will turn their mourning into joy, I will … gladden them after their sorrows.

PALM SUNDAY

MT 21:1-11; IS 50:4-7; PS 22:8-9, 17-20, 23-24; PHIL 2:6-11
MT 26:14-27:66 (YEAR A)
MK 14:1- 15:47 (YEAR B)
LK 19:28-40, 22:14-23:56 (YEAR C)

And when he entered Jerusalem the whole city was shaken ...

Perhaps the most mystifying question on our minds when it comes to Palm Sunday is this: how could the crowd, so quickly and violently, turn against the Savior they once revered? Let's examine the passage. The people who accompanied Jesus did not stroll into Jerusalem smiling and introducing him to everyone as their new buddy. The scene, we might imagine, was almost chaotic: an entourage of followers exhibiting adulation that bordered on fanaticism. People were placing their cloaks on the road and cutting off tree branches and laying them down so that even the feet of the donkey upon which Jesus sat should not touch the ground. They kept *crying out:* "Blessed is he who comes in the name of the Lord!" Whatever emotional state the people were in, and however passionately they felt about Jesus in that moment, it was enough that "the whole city was shaken." In other words, those witnessing this crowd were confused, unnerved, distressed ... and even afraid. What they were *not* is peaceful and joyful. Something was "off." And whatever it was, it was enough to affect not just a few onlookers, but rather "the *whole* city."

So what was the thing that was "off"? Scripture offers us a clue by what happens next:

> *[They] asked, "Who is this?" And the crowds replied, "This is Jesus the prophet, from Nazareth in Galilee."*

The revering crowds, who were just moments before proclaiming, "Hosanna to the Son of David," now could not correctly answer the question that Jesus asks all of us: "Who do you say that I am?" (Mt 16:15). They understood him to be a great prophet, like Elijah, but evidently not the Messiah, of whom the great prophets foretold. And without that understanding of Jesus proclaimed not just with our lips but also with our hearts, our faith will be built not on solid rock, but rather on sand. So for those accompanying Jesus in his procession into Jerusalem that day, "the winds blew and buffeted the house. And it collapsed and was completely ruined" (Mt 7:27).

> *One of the Twelve, who was called Judas Iscariot, went to the chief priests and said, "What are you willing to give me if I hand him over to you?"*

And now we contrast the people accompanying Jesus into Jerusalem with Judas Iscariot, the friend and betrayer of Jesus. So why did his "house" collapse? Why was his faith in Jesus "completely ruined"? Was it that he, too, did not know in the depths of his heart who Jesus really was? Sadly, incredulously, that is not likely. We cannot extend the same excuse to Judas as we can to the crowd. Judas, after all, walked closely with Jesus — for years. He witnessed the miracles; he even performed them himself in Jesus's name (Mk 6:13). So what happened to Judas? It seems that the seeds sown in his heart were planted among "thorns":

> *The seed sown among thorns is the one who hears the word, but then worldly anxiety and the lure of riches choke the word and it bears no fruit* … (Mt 13:22)

What does this tell us? It tells us that, like Judas, we do not have the benefit of explaining away our transgressions and betrayals with the excuse of being counted among those on the path upon which the seed fell, as was the case with the crowd:

> *The seed sown on the path is the one who hears the word of the kingdom without understanding it, and the evil one comes and steals away what was sown in his heart …* (Mt 13:19)

Unlike the crowd, we *do* understand the word. We *do* know exactly who Jesus is. It is a mystifying and incredible mercy that the Lord should have given the honor of this understanding and knowledge to us, weak and undeserving creatures that we are. Dare I say, this says something to us about our growth in humility, or at least our striving for it. *However.* Judas proves to us today that a gift received from the Lord can just as easily be lost, and that it is up to us to "use it or lose it." Frankly, I find that prospect frightening, precisely because I know how weak I am. It is this knowledge that causes me to shake, just like the whole city of Jerusalem was shaken the day Jesus entered their city gates. But fortunately, the Lord has also taught us a thing or two about how to form our hearts into ones that are rich with fertile soil, so that his word does not get snatched away, fallen away, or choked away. Instead, if we do as Jesus tells us, we will have a heart that "bears fruit and yields a hundred or sixty or thirtyfold" (Mt 13:23).

So what does Jesus ask of us?

"Jesus has many lovers of his heavenly kingdom, but few cross-bearers ... Many love Jesus when all goes well with them, and praise him when he does them a favor; but if Jesus conceals himself and leaves them for a little while, they fall to complaining or become depressed. They who love Jesus purely for himself and not for their own sake bless him in all trouble and anguish as well as in time of consolation." — Thomas à Kempis

One year when my family went on vacation, my plan was to stock up on plenty of ice cream for us to enjoy as a special treat. The store was having a "buy one, get one" sale, so it was perfect, because I love coffee ice cream, and my kids enjoy cookies and cream! My plan was all set. The problem was, guess what flavor the store was out of? Coffee. Now my initial reaction was disappointment. Who wouldn't get disappointed over ice cream? But then I had my *second* reaction, which was to remember to give God praise and thanks in *all* things! This little splinter of an offering was a way I could pray without ceasing for the much more difficult circumstances in my life; a way I could help Jesus in *his* job ... which is to "take care of everything." Friends, if we want the word planted in the rich soil of our hearts, then we need do nothing more than to accept whatever Jesus sends! It is true, sometimes what he sends will involve hairshirts, fasting, persecutions or even viruses ... but sometimes, it really is just about ice cream. Sometimes, Jesus just wants us to practice with the little things, because if we can't do that, how can we expect ourselves to take on the much greater crosses in life? Now don't get me wrong. I am the last person who wants to "practice" for a big cross! The possibility of a future big cross sounds terrifying. But the point of practicing now with things like ice cream is so that we are *not* terrified of ... whatever Jesus may send. And do you know what? That actually sounds ... pretty amazing. The disciples had their "faith in [Jesus] shaken," and they all "left him and fled." But what did Jesus do when he experienced anxiety in the Garden? He turned to the Father in prayer. He told the Father he didn't like it, he didn't want it ... but then he said:

Your will be done!

May we too turn to the Father as our *first* reaction when hardships come our way. It is okay to let him know we don't like the plan very much ... but then, let's smile. It is our very acceptance that will be just the "help" Jesus needs to take care of *everything*.

MONDAY OF HOLY WEEK

(IS 42:1-7; PS 27:1-3, 13-14; JN 12:1-11)

Mary took a liter of costly perfumed oil made from genuine aromatic nard and anointed the feet of Jesus and dried them with her hair.

The resurrection of Jesus, which we will celebrate just six days from now — and in reality, we celebrate every time we attend Mass — is such an enormous deal in Christianity that it is, in fact, what our whole faith is based on. Without that resurrection event, we would have no Christian religion, no Messiah to follow. Every miracle Jesus performed, every good work, every manifestation of mercy and kindness, would have been either washed away in the forgotten annals of history, or chalked up to his being another great prophet or spiritual leader. But just not explained by his being the Son of God.

So understandably, the Church places heavy emphasis on Christ's passion, death, and resurrection. It is the reason salvation is available to us. The thing is … Christ's resurrection is *such* a big deal, that we can overlook what a big deal Lazarus's resurrection was to his friends and family just six days prior. When Mary pours the perfumed oil that is worth nearly one year's salary upon the Lord's feet, we might think, "Wow, that was one devoted woman." But this act of generosity on Mary's part is more than just due to her being Jesus's number one fan. Jesus gave Mary her brother back! She owes Jesus her life! Or at least, her whole life is his now, as a gift in response to the incredible miracle that Jesus has procured for her.

> *When Martha heard that Jesus was coming, she went to meet him; but Mary sat at home.* (Jn 11:20)

After Lazarus had died, and Martha went to meet Jesus, why do we suppose Mary stayed home? Did she simply not hear that Jesus was in town, while Martha, her sister, who was grieving right alongside her, did hear but simply failed to mention it? Or perhaps Mary was too overcome with grief to get out of bed? Was she angry at Jesus for not coming sooner and was now giving him the cold shoulder? These possible scenarios are all unlikely. Let's remember that Mary was the one who "sat beside the Lord at his feet listening to him speak" (Lk 10: 39), an act that was remarkable for a first-century Palestinian Jewish woman. Mary was the one who was most prepared for this heartbreaking moment in which she lost her brother; she would have received and absorbed every word the Master spoke with a heart that was rich and fertile. So what would Mary have been doing, staying home, while her sister Martha went out to meet the Master by herself? Mary, undoubtedly, would have been *praying*. But for what? Her brother was gone now, and having not been able to imagine the possibility of his resurrection, it is unlikely she would have been asking the Father to bring him back to life. Equally unlikely is that she would have been asking "why," as she would have been a woman full of trust in the Lord. When she finally does meet with Jesus, she simply says, "Lord, if you had been here…" (Jn 11:32). But she does not ask, "Why didn't you come sooner?" So what would Mary have been saying to the Father in her overwhelming grief, as she stayed back at home without her sister?

> *Though an army encamp against me, my heart will not fear; Though war be waged upon me, even then will I trust.*

Mary, quite undoubtedly, would have been giving God praise and thanks in all things. She would have made the decision to *increase* her trust, at the very moment when every fiber of her being was tempted to throw it away. And it would have been this trust that would set the scene for what happens next:

> *Jesus said to her, "Did I not tell you that if you believe you will see the glory of God?" .... And Jesus raised his eyes and said, "Father, I thank you for hearing me ..." And when he had said this, he cried out in a loud voice, "Lazarus, come out!"* (Jn 11: 40-43)

It is true, Jesus prophesied the miracle he would procure days before he was to procure it. But it is also true that Jesus wills to be unable to heal and cure unless there is someone "raising arms in supplication" to ask for it (Father Gabriel of St. Mary Magdalene, *Divine Intimacy*). Without the faith of the people, Jesus will not — and in this sense, *cannot* — perform his miracles, as we see in the case of the people of his own hometown. So when we read about this beautiful scene in which Lazarus is raised from the dead, and our hearts are filled with gratitude to God ... let's realize, we also have Mary to thank.

> *"Why was this oil not sold for three hundred days' wages and given to the poor?" He said this not because he cared about the poor but because he was a thief ...*

And so Mary, filled with gratitude and trust beyond all telling, is now filled with the Spirit and is inspired to give the most costly and precious item she owns, and pour it upon the Lord's feet. It is a gesture that says that everything she has to give is his — her whole heart — and that what she has is reserved for the lowest place: the Savior's feet. She is overcome by love. And in this precious and tender moment ... Judas sees red.

Ah Judas. He has really managed to become the killjoy at every party. But friends, this is what happens when we let our ugly side take over. Because the reality is, we all have a little Judas in us. Oh, maybe we're not thieves or betrayers ... but we all have our "thing." And you know your personal "thing" is starting to come out when the people around you begin to feel anxious in your presence. Ugh.

Years ago, my husband and I were planning a getaway, one which I was really looking forward to. Between soccer, boy scouts, volunteering, and work, we had been spending our days going in different directions, so I was excited to have some quality time to ourselves. But then people we had not invited … invited themselves to come along! You can imagine my reaction to that unwelcome news. I was not one for unpleasant, awkward conversations, so I decided the best course of action was to stew with it in the isolation of my brain, and keep my mouth shut. The keeping my mouth shut part was a good idea … except that my motivation wasn't out of Christian charity, but rather, fear of broaching and mishandling an uncomfortable subject. So, as is the way whenever anybody stews over something, I spent the whole trip in a bad mood, making everyone around me anxious. It's not that I didn't have reason to be disappointed or even upset. But I did not bring what was troubling me to the Lord, I didn't ask him to show me what he was doing in all this, and I didn't ask him how he wanted me to handle things. Like Judas, I made it about one thing ("not because he cared about the poor…"), when it was really about something else ("but because he was a thief…"). How differently things could have turned out for Judas if he had just come to Jesus with what was heavy on his heart. He could have had the oppression of jealousy, anger, fear … all lifted, perhaps even in an instant. Judas could have been set *free.*

> *I formed you, and set you as a covenant of the people, a light for the nations, to open the eyes of the blind, to bring out prisoners from confinement, and from the dungeon, those who live in darkness.*

If temptation strikes us at every corner, threatening to bring out our inner ugly, let's bring it to the Lord instead. There are really only two ways things can go: either in a downward spiral, or in a letting go that sets us free to live in the peace and joy of Christ's love. If we choose option one, we have no further to look than to Judas to see how the story ends. Let us choose option two, and, like Mary, set everything we have to give at the feet of Jesus. In return, let us receive freedom and healing at the foot of the cross.

The LORD is my life's refuge; of whom should I be afraid?

TUESDAY OF HOLY WEEK

(IS 49:1-6; PS 71:1-6, 15,17; JN 13:21-38)

Jesus was deeply troubled and testified, "Amen, amen, I say to you, one of you will betray me."

And so we enter into this ominous scene, just moments before Satan "entered" Judas, but after Satan had already "induced" him to hand Jesus over (Jn 13:2). The devil is lurking around this very first Mass offered in salvation history. If this sounds creepy, let's realize that the devil is lurking around *every* Mass that has been offered since that first one, throughout the whole world. But how is this possible? Is the Holy Mass not our refuge and our sanctuary? Our fortress within whose walls we shall not fear? Absolutely. But God will only "conceal in the shadow of his arm" those whose hearts seek refuge in him. It is souls who come to Mass strictly out of routine — or worse, hypocrisy — that the devil lies in wait to snatch away, lest they open their hearts to the floodgates of grace that is available to them, just one tiny crack away. Satan seeks to "induce" us with *distraction.* With *boredom.* With *doubt.* With *ruminating.* With *anxiety.* With *anger.* With *unforgiveness.* With *pride.* And with each temptation we succumb to, we finally get to the point where we can no longer *see.* Even when Jesus himself stands right before us. Such is the case with Judas.

"Master, who is it?" Jesus answered, "It is the one to whom I hand the morsel after I have dipped it."

Peter prompts John, Jesus's "beloved," to find out who this betrayer among them will be. At this point, Peter decides for certain that it is not going to be him, and it is not going to be John. Whoever else he might have ruled out, Scripture does not tell us. John asks Jesus, in a whisper, we might imagine, so as to keep it between themselves. Now here is where it gets interesting. Jesus doesn't reply, "It's going to be Judas! Judas is the one!" Rather, he offers a rather cryptic answer about dipping bread and handing it over, almost as if he's leaving clues for John to solve the puzzle. But why? Why shroud the truth in such mystery? Why not plainly speak the culprit's name? Well, we know for certain it is not because Jesus is playing games. This is not a "game" in any sense of the word. This is life and death.

Perhaps Jesus does not speak the name of Judas because the moment Satan would enter him, he would cease to be Judas. At least the Judas they knew. If Jesus would have named anyone to John in that moment he asked him who it was that would betray him, Jesus would have most accurately replied, "Satan." It would have been an answer that John could not possibly have understood until much later.

When Jesus says to his betrayer, "What you are going to do, do quickly," we now understand why Judas took no time to hesitate or pretend or excuse; rather, he "took the morsel and left at once." It is the devil himself who has snatched that morsel of bread and cannot leave fast enough to execute his plan. The person of Judas, for all intents and purposes, is gone.

Jesus answered, "Will you lay down your life for me? Amen, amen, I say to you, the cock will not crow before you deny me three times."

And now we turn to the man formerly known as Simon. This is Jesus's "Peter," the man Jesus has named and claimed as his own. This time Jesus offers no clues shrouded in mystery about the failure that lies ahead for Peter. Jesus simply tells him plainly and straight to his face what is to occur. This is the man who prompted John to ask Jesus who the betrayer would be; what must have been going through his mind when Jesus says that Peter himself would deny him three times? Let's remember, when Jesus said to Judas to do what he had to do quickly, "none of those reclining at table realized why he said this to him." Did Peter think now that Jesus is suggesting he would be the betrayer? Whatever Peter thought, Jesus is pretty blunt; there is no question as to who or what he means. But why such "straight talk" when it comes to Peter, as opposed to the enigmatic mystery reserved for Judas? Because this time, Jesus is not dealing with Satan, the deceiver. He is dealing with Peter, his impetuous and weak friend. Peter would deny him, it is true, but it would be out of weakness, and not malice. And Jesus could work with that. If we are honest with him about our weakness, mystifyingly, Jesus will love us all the more for it. Rather than push us further away from him, our very weakness will draw us close — snuggled right up against the refuge of his merciful heart. Jesus loves us to remain little and at his feet, so sometimes he will allow us a fall or two to knock us off our high horse. Peter's denial certainly would have wounded the Sacred Heart ... but more than the wound he experienced, Jesus would have felt joy, knowing that Peter's fall from grace would be for a greater good. Later, as Pope, it would be these denials that Peter would never forget. He would never think of himself as "better" than anyone, chosen or not. He would have taken the lowest place of humility, despite being the one appointed to lead the Church all over the world.

> *He made of me a sharp-edged sword and concealed me in the shadow of his arm. He made me a polished arrow, in his quiver he hid me ...You are my servant, he said to me. It is too little, he says, for you to be my servant ... I will make you a light to the nations, that my salvation may reach to the ends of the earth.*

Let's now contrast Peter's story with the rest of Judas's:

> *Then Judas, his betrayer, seeing that Jesus had been condemned, deeply regretted what he had done ...* (Mt 27:3)

Evidently when Satan satisfactorily accomplished his mission for which he had employed Judas, he was now done with him. So he simply departs, leaving Judas to rot in his own misery. And it is once Satan is gone, that Judas can now clearly see the horror of what he has done. Such is the way with any sin we choose to engage in, regardless of how big or small it is: there is a certain blindness moments before we commit it, and a definitive, crushing awareness moments after. Satan leaves us alone, at least temporarily, once he has accomplished his mission. Which is why he works so hard at Mass, the very place of lifesaving, merciful grace. And yet if we come to Mass for refuge ... then we have nothing to fear. In fact, it will seem to us as though the devil is not even there, because all we will experience is the choir of angels and saints surrounding us, glorifying God in an exuberance of peaceful joy! We can almost feel sorry for Judas in all his bitter regret; perhaps we can even recognize him in ourselves. But that should compel us all the more to trust in God's mercy, and to seek his refuge. Jesus does not ask us to do everything "right." He just asks us to *try*. His grace will fill in the rest if we humbly recognize our powerlessness and trust in his mercy and love.

> *And I am made glorious in the sight of the LORD, and my God is now my strength!*

WEDNESDAY OF HOLY WEEK

(IS 50:4-9; PS 69:8-10, 21-22, 31,33-34; MT 26:14-25)

Then Judas, his betrayer, said in reply, "Surely it is not I, Rabbi?"

What do we suppose is going through Judas's mind at this moment? Here, Jesus has made a clear, prophetic announcement that one of the disciples would betray him … and Judas acts just as shocked as all the other disciples. Does he think he could "fool" Jesus by pretending it would not be him? Maybe he thinks of Jesus as one of those self-proclaimed psychics who shroud their foretelling in vague clues because they can only "see" bits and pieces into the future, but not the whole picture? Or perhaps he really does believe that Jesus knows darn well it would be Judas, but if he could at least fool the rest of the disciples, he would still have a shot at keeping his thirty pieces of silver? Scripture does not reveal to us what was going through Judas's mind. But there is one other option that could explain what made him act just as shocked as the other disciples in hearing that one of them would betray Jesus: perhaps Judas really does not know that he would be the one.

My mother was one of six siblings — all of whom married and had kids of their own — so I grew up with lots of extended family. One of my fondest childhood memories was going to my grandmother's house for family gatherings, surrounded by all my cousins. Of course, there were a few gatherings that were *not* so delightful to remember; specifically, the times I felt picked on by the other kids, as is the way with normal childhood rivalries. Recently I was in conversation with one of my cousins, reminiscing about old times. When I warmly shared with her that my favorite memories were of all of us gathered at Grandma's, she looked at me, cocked her head to the side, and flatly announced, "Those weren't *my* favorite memories. You were always such a bully." My cousin was not angry; actually, she was laughing about it now … but one can imagine my shock. *Me*?? The bully? I was the victim! Days later, her comment stayed with me because I honestly had no idea what she was talking about. Then I remembered … the times I was relieved when she was being murmured about and I was not … the times I said nothing in her defense … and, I imagined, the times that I quite possibly joined in the conspiring against her, times erased long ago from my memory, but seared painfully in hers. I called her to apologize for any pain I had caused her … and she lovingly forgave me, saying it was a long time ago. I never even knew.

Such, perhaps, was the disposition of Judas in the midst of this shocking revelation from Jesus. Perhaps he truly did not see himself as a "betrayer." Perhaps he only viewed things from his own perspective — that of "victim" — whose Messiah was not carrying out the plan he had promised, at least not in the way or in the timetable Judas had expected. Bafflingly, it is possible Judas might even have thought he was doing Jesus a favor — helping push his mission along. In fact, he was. Just not in the way Judas intended. If only Judas could have found it in his heart to acknowledge his betrayal to the Lord and say, "I'm sorry." It's true, "sorry" wouldn't have "cut it." But Jesus would have forgiven him anyway.

> *The Son of Man indeed goes, as it is written of him, but woe to that man by whom the Son of Man is betrayed. It would be better for that man if he had never been born.*

HOLY THURSDAY

(EX 12:1-14; PS 116:1-2, 12-19; 1 COR 11:23-26; JN 13:1-17; 31-35)

Jesus answered and said to him, "What I am doing, you do not understand now, but you will understand later."

Well, doesn't this single statement sum up the Christian life? When the Holy Spirit acts in our lives, *sometimes* it is a great joy and obvious blessing ... but very often, the actions of the Spirit are shrouded in mystery. That is a charitable way of saying we often don't like very much what God has planned for our lives. In fact, to our way of thinking, often God's plan does not even seem to make much sense. X seems that it would have been the most fitting, logical ending to our difficulty; and instead, God chooses Y. But why? Why would God choose the most baffling of outcomes, the one that tests our faith? For two reasons, the first of which should be obvious to us by the very question just posed. The primary reason God hides from us the understanding of his workings is to prompt us to *trust.*

Peter said to him, "You will never wash my feet."

Peter's first reaction, like that of so many of us, is to assume, in his lack of understanding, that there must be some mistake. *This can't be. Jesus can't mean this.* So his initial response to Jesus is essentially, "I can't accept this."

Jesus answered him, "Unless I wash you, you will have no inheritance with me."

Peter still does not understand; Jesus's reply still does not answer the question of "why." But now, Peter is beginning to open his heart enough to meet him with a compromise:

Simon Peter said to him, "Master, then not only my feet, but my hands and head as well."

How often do we compromise with Jesus as well? "I'll do this *if*." But Jesus doesn't work with compromises. He has no need to make deals because he is already doing what he knows is best for us. To compromise with our demands would be to give us less than what is best. It is like a parent offering their child filet mignon, but then "compromising" with a hot dog because it is the only "beef" the child is willing to try. The God who loves us knows the better option for our lives. We just have to trust him, even if what he is offering is something we don't like now but will learn to love later.

Jesus said to him, "Whoever has bathed has no need except to have his feet washed, for he is clean all over..."

Jesus still does not explain to Peter why he must wash his feet, but he does point out the lack of logic in Peter's reasoning. When my oldest son was little, he had a hard time swallowing pills. In fact, it was such an ordeal for him, he would rather suffer through a fever than take some Tylenol. One day, at his annual check-up, the nurse cheerfully announced that one of the usual routine shots was now available in pill form. She thought she was delivering to us good news! But my son's face fell in horror. Beyond all logic, he opted for the painful shot. He just could not get past his own reasoning to see what was actually best.

...he said to them, "Do you realize what I have done for you? ... I have given you a model to follow, so that as I have done for you, you should also do."

It is not until Peter consents — not until he accepts the will of the Master, even though he does not like it or understand it — that the understanding comes. Jesus has humbled himself to wash Peter's feet in order to model the behavior that he wants Peter to follow. But why not simply say, "Peter, I want you to wash other people's feet?" Why must Jesus be the "model" of such behavior? We can imagine a number of reasons, not the least of which is that Peter could never have the excuse, *Easy for the Master to say. He doesn't have to do it.* Friends, whatever it is the Lord asks us to endure, let's first and foremost realize that it is nothing Jesus has not endured himself. Pain? Check. Humiliation? Check. Rejection? Check. Sorrow? Check. Let's also realize that if he's asking us to undergo that which he has endured himself, he has given us both a model to follow in the midst of our trials, as well as a sneak peek into how the story ends. Let's start with that "sneak peek." Jesus's story does not end with pain, humiliation, rejection, and sorrow. It ends with "all things work for good for those who love God and are called according to his purpose" (Rom 8:28). And herein lies the second reason that God would choose the most baffling of outcomes, the one that tests our faith. Because if right now we are experiencing pain, humiliation, rejection, or sorrow, that is a sure sign to us that the "outcome" has not come yet at all. We are still in the *middle* of the story; we have not yet arrived at the final chapter. That final chapter, if we persevere in trust, has a *happy* and *glorious* ending, one that includes "plans for [our] welfare and not for woe, so as to give [us] a future of hope" (Jer 29:11). So let's hold on to hope "a little while" longer (Jn 16:16).

But what is the model Jesus gives us to follow as we await that happy ending that is full of hope? He does not model asking why, he does not model resisting acceptance, he does not model bargaining or compromising with the Father; rather, Jesus models seeking the Father's hand in all our circumstances. Jesus does indeed want us to grow in trust, by accepting that which he sends, even before we understand. But he knows how weak and little we are, and so he also wills to give us the encouragement we need to persevere. He may not reveal to us now how the story ends — we just have to take his word for it that what we "do not understand now, [we] will understand later." But if we ask him to show us that he is in our midst, that he has not forgotten our pain or our difficulty, and for the "proof" that he is taking care of things, he surely will.

Recently, one of my adult children was going through something very difficult. I was miles away, unable to be there for her. But a sibling decided on the spur of the moment that morning, for the first time ever, to take a "mental health" day from work (code for: he didn't feel like going in). Because of that, he was able to provide his sister with the company and comfort she needed, so she would not be alone in her pain. It was the providence of God, guiding them through their circumstance, whispering in my son's ear to stay home. To quote the famous children's series, *Flat Stanley*:

> "...things often happen without there seeming to be a reason, and then something else happens, and suddenly the first thing seems to have had a purpose after all."

What seemed to make no sense to Peter on that Holy Thursday as Jesus washed his feet, would make all the sense in the world by the time their Passover meal was complete. Jesus had instituted the Sacrament of the Eucharist; his gift of service would be to offer his very flesh for the life of the world.

GOOD FRIDAY

(IS 52:13-53:12; PS 31:2, 6, 12-13, 15-17, 25; HEB 10:16-25; HEB 4:14-16; 5:7-9; JN 18:1-19:42)

So Pilate came out to them and said, "What charge do you bring against this man?" They answered and said to him, "If he were not a criminal, we would not have handed him over to you."

The Jews cannot even reply to Pilate's question with a precise answer. It seems they can't get their story straight; everyone's a little fuzzy on exactly what the charge against Jesus even is. And such is the way when we do not understand our own actions; we can't explain them logically to anyone else.

Since he could not get a straight answer out of those who wished to convict Jesus, Pilate now turns to Jesus for a clear answer:

"Your own nation and the chief priests handed you over to me. What have you done?" Jesus answered, "My kingdom does not belong to this world."

Pilate definitely does not receive a clear answer from Jesus either to the question, "What have you done?" But rather than being confused or fuzzy about his own understanding, if anything, Jesus seems to be inciting and instigating the violence that is about to be perpetrated upon him. It's like he *wants* to bring it on. And … in a sense, he does. As weak as his flesh was in the Garden of

Gethsemane, so now his Spirit has been made all the stronger by the fortification of grace the Father has bestowed upon him. Jesus has gone from dragging his feet in distress and anxiety … to peaceful acceptance … to willing embrace. He is not simply past not liking his cross. He has moved to *loving* it, *desiring* it, *longing* for it … not simply out of acceptance of his Father's will, but because it has become his own will too. And not just his divine will, but a will that comes fully from his humanity as well. Friends, this is mind boggling. And it teaches us an important lesson today. Jesus did not carry his cross, endure torture, and willingly die for our sins simply because he is the great *I AM*; that is to say, because God can do anything. Let's keep in mind — in a mystery we could never fully comprehend — Jesus the Nazorean was also *fully human.* Yes, his divinity willed to carry that cross, longed for it, thirsted for it … but so did his *humanity*. So what does this tell us? It tells us that it is also possible for *us* to go past resistance, not just to peaceful acceptance, but to a thirst for a will we could never imagine wanting. Not without God's grace, certainly. But it does not take being divine in order to partake in Christ's same longing. Why? Because every time we receive Jesus in his word and particularly in his Eucharist, we receive *him*; quite literally. Jesus enters in, and we are transformed:

> "By eating the Body and drinking the Blood of Christ in the Eucharist, we become united to the person of Christ through his humanity. "Whoever eats my flesh and drinks my blood remains in me and I in him" (Jn 6:56). In being united to the humanity of Christ, we are at the same time united to his divinity" (www.usccb.org/eucharist).

So Jesus does not answer Pilate's question with a straight answer. He does not say, "Well, they're charging me with such and such, but I didn't do it." Instead, he gives a rather cryptic answer about his Kingdom, and then ends with, "Everyone who belongs to the truth listens to my voice." But do you know what? Incredibly, something about that reply which does not answer the question resonates with Pilate. He goes back to the Jews and says to them:

I find no guilt in him.

But why? Why advocate for this man Pilate does not even know and who has not even spoken clearly in his own defense? Evidently, Pilate himself is one of those Jesus described as *listening* to his voice! Incredibly, something in Pilate recognizes the truth in Jesus's words. In this moment, Pilate stands at a crossroads: will he choose to belong to the Truth, or will he choose to belong to Deceit? We are on the edge of our seats now …

Do you want me to release to you the King of the Jews?

Pilate comes so close. This is the moment where Pilate could have gone down in history as one of the greatest Christian converts ever recorded. This could have been his "Saul to Paul" moment! But … alas. He is not ready. We can recognize the tangible struggle within himself; on the one hand, doing the job he has been told to do, and yet, on the other hand, having recognized Truth, knowing his job is betraying what he now knows to be true:

Look, I am bringing him out to you, so that you may know that I find no guilt in him.

Take him yourselves and crucify him. I find no guilt in him.

Pilate said to [Jesus], "Do you not speak to me? Do you not know that I have power to release you and I have power to crucify you?"

Consequently, Pilate tried to release him … And he said to the Jews, "Behold, your king!"

These are Pilate's last-ditch but feeble efforts to free the Savior of the world. But of course, such freedom was not to be. We can almost feel the heaviness and distress in Pilate's heart when he beseeches the Jews:

Shall I crucify your king?

Pilate knows in his heart a grave injustice is being committed before him, and at his hand. It is the very reason he announces in futility, "I am innocent of this man's blood" (Mt 27:24), as if saying so would make it so. But as we well know, only God's word has the power to do that. For the rest of us weak and sinful creatures … actions speak louder than words.

So Pontius Pilate, despite his words declaring Christ's innocence, and despite being the one who protested Jesus's crucifixion the most — even more than Jesus's own disciples — has gone down in history as the sole culprit under whom Jesus "suffered." Now, it is true that Scripture scholars disagree as to whether Pilate's culpability is one of weakness or one of malice (Daniel J. Harrington, S.J., *Sacra Pagina: The Gospel of Matthew*); and yet, it seems Pilate did *try* to do the right thing. Isn't that all Jesus asks of us? The thing is, when Jesus asks us to "try," he is talking about the things which are beyond our control, the things over which we are powerless, the things we can *only* do with his grace. This includes things like forgiving offenses, overcoming temptation, growing in virtue, striving to trust. But if my toddler is running into the street and I "try" to stop him by calling out his name, but do not physically go after him for fear of getting hit by a car myself, that would hardly be considered fulfilling my responsibility as a parent. Such was the "effort" of Pilate. If his responsibility was to carry out justice, then the reality is, he really did not even try. It seems the risk to himself was just too great. And that is why, in the end, the Church's Creed points singularly to Pilate as the one "under" whom Jesus suffered.

One final note. The reality is, there is *nothing* Pilate could have said or done that would have changed a thing. Jesus's crucifixion was the will of God after all. But that does not mean the Lord did not want Pilate to try anyway. And we must keep this in mind when it comes to our own regrets in life. "I should have done this … If only I'd done that." There really is no "I should have" or "if only" because nothing we do could ever override the will of God. If in the past, we didn't listen to the voice of Truth … then let us simply and peacefully begin today. Just like he did for St. Paul, Jesus will take the most regrettable of our actions and transform them into something new, something better than we ever imagined, provided that we turn our lives over to him. Our Heavenly Father makes "all things work for good for those who love God and are called according to his purpose" (Rom 8:28).

HOLY SATURDAY EASTER VIGIL

(PS 16:5,8-11; EX 14:15-15:1; IS 55:1-11; PS 19:8-11; IS 12:2-6; MT 28:1-10)

The guards were shaken with fear of him and became like dead men.

So this angel appears out of nowhere, sitting upon the giant rock which had moments before been displaced from its position that had enclosed Jesus's tomb. Whether the angel's "rolling back" of the stone was the literal interpretation of events, or whether it was merely Matthew's literary style to express that the rock was shaken loose in the earthquake, we do not know. What we do know is that it was the hand of God who set that rolling stone in motion — whether by an act of nature, or by an act of the supernatural. As far as the angel … it is difficult for us to imagine precisely what Matthew means when he says his appearance was "like lightening." Does he mean the angel came suddenly, "quick as a flash"? Or does he mean that he appeared with a beam of bright light? Were the clothes he was wearing "white as snow" because of the light that surrounded him? Or did the angel carry a much more natural appearance, that of a "sparkling" clean messenger of God, but one human in appearance? Matthew does not specify in such detail, perhaps because he was not there. Perhaps Mary Magdalene and the other Mary simply could not adequately describe the indescribable to Matthew. How does one adequately describe a glorious sunset to a person who has spent his entire life in a cave? Such is the chasm between heaven and earth. We live but a shadow and foretaste of what is to come; words could never adequately express what only the spirit can see.

Whatever appearance that angel took, and however that stone was rolled aside, it was enough to frighten the guards to such a degree that they "became like dead men." What a strange way to phrase it. "Shaken" with fear we understand. "Paralyzed" with fear we comprehend. "Trembling," "overcome," "panicked," are all apt descriptions of a fear we can envision for ourselves in the most frightening of circumstances. But under what terrifying circumstance would we become *like dead men*? Just one really.

> *That is why I told you that you will die in your sins. For if you do not believe that I AM, you will die in your sins.* (Jn 8:24)

Perhaps, in that singular moment when the angel appeared "like lightening," the guards, for the first time in their lives, saw clearly every sin they had ever committed before God, lit up in a flash before their very eyes, all at once.

> … *the LORD is clear, enlightening the eye.*

That which they had previously been blind to now stood glaringly apparent right before them.

> … *the LORD cast … a glance that threw [them] into a panic …*

To one who has never repented, never examined their sins, never tried to make amends or to grow in virtue … that illumination of conscience at the horror of what one has done would be enough to strike one down as if dead.

> *The stone that the builders rejected has become the cornerstone … The one who falls on this stone will be dashed to pieces; and it will crush anyone on whom it falls …* (Mt 21: 42,44)

Now we turn to the women, who also encounter the very same angel, the one who is "white as snow," and whose appearance is "like lightning":

> *Then the angel said to the women in reply, "Do not be afraid! … go*

> *quickly and tell his disciples, 'he has been raised from the dead, and he is going before you to Galilee'..."*

Why didn't the women become "like dead men"? Well, it would follow, that if the guards became like dead men because they had never examined their sins before, for the women, it would have been just the opposite. These are women who would have already experienced a conversion moment, and in fact, spent their days prayerfully in continual reflection, both repenting of their past transgressions and striving to do better. The appearance of the angel would not have caused the shock to their system the way it did to the guards, because they had already spent their days and nights preparing for this moment.

> *Then they went away quickly from the tomb, fearful yet overjoyed, and ran to announce this to his disciples.*

This is not to say, however, that the sight of the angel did not instill a certain fear in them. If that were not the case, there would have been no need for the angel to extol them: "Be not afraid!" So in what way were these women afraid? Unlike the guards, the fear that these women experienced would have manifested itself in awe and trembling at the mighty power of God. In other words, the fear these women experienced would have been a *Fear of the Lord.* But isn't this a good thing? If they were experiencing a rightly ordered fear, why does the angel tell them, "Do not be afraid"? Because there is a *way* in which Fear of the Lord should manifest itself in our hearts, and it's not by panic, anxiety, distress, or agitation.

> *And behold, Jesus met them on their way and greeted them. They approached, embraced his feet, and did him homage. Then Jesus said to them, "Do not be afraid. Go tell my brothers to go to Galilee, and there they will see me."*

Now this is odd. The angel already gave the ladies such and such instructions about telling the disciples to meet Jesus in Galilee, and they immediately go, in obedience, to do precisely as he says. So why did the Master appear to them to repeat the exact same instructions? Was he worried they would get distracted and forget? Was it so they would not later doubt that what they heard from the angel had been commanded by the Lord? Scripture does not reveal Jesus's reasons to us. But what we do know is that the first words Jesus says to these women are the very same first words the angel said to them: "Do not be afraid." In other words, it seems the first "Do not be afraid" from the angel did not really take. Likely their hearts were still racing, the women were presumably shaking and nervous … and this was not the way that Jesus would have wanted his good news to be presented to his disciples. He would not have wanted the two ladies agitated, talking over each other excitedly or hysterically. What did Jesus want for them? He wanted *peace.* It is certain that what the angel did not provide for the two women, would have been granted them by Jesus instantly, at his word.

> … *my word shall not return to me void, but shall do my will, achieving the end for which I sent it.*

Jesus does indeed elicit in us an awe and wonder in the Fear of the Lord that we experience in his presence, but it is a fear that is also accompanied by a deep and abiding peace, surrounded by the rays of his unimaginable love and mercy. This is what it means to have a rightly ordered Fear of the Lord, and it is in this disposition that Jesus wants us carrying out his commands. Further, when we are in a rightly ordered relationship with him, we follow those commands not because we have to, but because we *want* to. Our task ceases to be a thankless, joyless obligation, but becomes our greatest pleasure and a genuine honor. Friends, this is why it is so important, in the words of Father Jacques Philippe, to seek and maintain peace as our *primary* obligation as Christians. From this disposition of peace, we are truly free to both discern and carry out God's will.

> *O LORD, my allotted portion and my cup, you it is who hold fast my lot. I set the LORD ever before me; with him at my right hand I shall not be disturbed.*

EASTER SUNDAY

(ACTS 10:34A, 37-43; PS 118:1-2, 16-17, 22-23; COL 3:1-4; JN 20:1-9)

Then the other disciple also went in, the one who had arrived at the tomb first, and he saw and believed. For they did not yet understand the Scripture that he had to rise from the dead.

When I was a young child, I was a pretty picky eater. I basically liked spaghetti or fried chicken for dinner, and if something else was being served, I generally turned my nose up at it. Having said that, my father had a rather sophisticated palate, so my mother would whip up on occasion some pretty exotic meals: liver, tripe, and my personal "favorite," tongue. Of all the dishes she would prepare to suit my father's taste, there was just one meal I would deign to eat: "Oxdale." Oxdale, so I thought, was the name of British beef stew. I never did mind the nights my mom made Oxdale because, throw it on top of a little rice, and it was actually pretty good. I ate my mom's Oxdale for years. Until one day ... I finally *understood*. My mother's "Oxdale" was in fact her Hispanic pronunciation of ... OX TAIL!!

John tells us when he saw the empty tomb, at this point he "did not yet understand the Scripture that [Jesus] had to rise from the dead." So what was it exactly that he now "saw and believed"? If it was belief in the resurrection, why does John then tell us in the verse immediately following this one that he "did not yet understand" that Jesus "had to rise from the dead"? What if instead, what he now believed to be true was that which Mary of Magdala had told him; that is, that "They have taken the Lord from the tomb"? Can we even imagine what lay in the hearts of Peter and John at that moment? Peter, already torn apart by his own cowardly denials of his friend, and despite his impetuous defense of Jesus when it came to severing the slave's ear, would have been so ashamed by his lacking courage to simply stand by Jesus when the Master needed him most. And now, Peter could not even protect Jesus's dead body from defilement. And John, the beloved, his own heart broken by the loss of his closest friend and father-figure/big brother, and now ... not even a grave where he could sit by his body for comfort, and to remember. The two friends could not have felt any more broken at any other moment in Christ's passion.

> *... seek what is above. Think of what is above, not of what is on earth. For you have died, and your life is hidden with Christ in God.*

It is scarcely possible to imagine what Peter and John would have felt in that moment. Because whereas we all certainly know the feeling of dejection, brokenness, and anguish over our circumstances, what sets us apart from the dejection, brokenness, and anguish that Peter and John experienced on that predawn Easter morning is that, unlike them, we have the *hope* of Christ. For Peter and John in that moment, when they "did not yet understand the resurrection," they had no hope left. For Peter and John, they knew the utter devastation of *despair.*

Friends, if we are experiencing right now our own predawn Easter morning, if that predawn has been going on a little too long ... let us hold onto the gift that the sunrise offers us: *he is risen! Alleluia!! Seek what is above!! Think of what is above!!* Let us think not of what is on earth, that which threatens to take away our hope. This world is passing; Jesus is forever! That is not to say that our time on earth will be met without pain, without sacrifice, without dejection, brokenness, or anguish. So what does it mean to "seek what is above" and "think of what is above," when our lives here below, at times, feel overwhelming, even more than we can bear? It means that instead of asking "Why," we ask the Lord to show us his hand in our circumstances. Instead of saying, "It's not fair," we say, "Jesus, I trust in You." It means instead of ruminating on the anger and resentment we feel over the pain others have caused us, we lift our hearts to God, offering hymns of praise and thanks. In this way, Jesus will restore our peace. Why is that so important? Because predawn does not last forever. One year from now, one month from now, one week from now, perhaps even one *day* from now ... this too shall pass. And when Easter morning finally comes for us, we won't be asking "Why?" any longer. "Why" will not even matter, because now we finally understand. So let's usher in that Easter morning by our patient acceptance and peaceful trust while we wait. Paradoxically, the more we accept our wait, the less painful our wait will be. In this way, Easter morning can be *every* morning for us in our hearts. Our trust makes our hope in Easter as good as done.

Jesus is risen indeed.

Finally, brothers, whatever is true, whatever is honorable, whatever is just, whatever is pure, whatever is lovely, whatever is gracious, if there is any excellence and if there is anything worthy of praise, think about these things. (Phil 4:8)

O Holy Family,
You who built a safe haven for the Word made flesh,
Teach us to build our homes into safe havens for our families.
May our families reflect the peace and love of Christ to all who enter,
And may our homes become a place of refuge in the Heart of Christ. Amen.

~C.T. & M.C.

ABOUT THE AUTHOR

M.C. Holbrook is a homeschooling mother of ten who writes reflections on daily Scripture readings as they apply to everyday life, both on a personal as well as global level. Originally from New York City, Holbrook received a Bachelor's degree in Human Development and Family Studies from Cornell University, and a Master's degree in School Counseling from New York University. At a time when the world has been falling into chaos, confusion, uncertainty, and division … she has found her rock, her fortress, her shield, and her peace right within the confines of her own heart and home … in the taste of heaven that is the word of God.